HIDDEN
HISTORY
of
CAPE COD

HIDDEN
HISTORY
of
CAPE COD

Theresa Mitchell Barbo

THE
History
PRESS

Published by The History Press
Charleston, SC 29403
www.historypress.net

Copyright © 2015 by Theresa Barbo

All rights reserved

First published 2015

Manufactured in the United States

ISBN 978.1.62619.710.7

Library of Congress Control Number: 2015936222

For Katherine Margaret and Thomas Daniel—
my two children who came of age on Cape Cod listening to history stories,
ever so patiently.

Love, Mum

Contents

CONTENTS

Acknowledgements

As a writer of narrative nonfiction history, I have depended on research libraries and the personal archives of individuals for unique materials with which to compose this book.

I am especially indebted to Bill Reidy of the Cape Cod chapter of the National Railroad Historical Society (capecodnrhs.org) for his generous support, including numerous photographs featured in this book. Carl Harrison reviewed the essay on railroads as well.

Amy Heller, administrator at the Historical Society of Old Yarmouth, procured a wonderful image of Stephen Sears for me. Meg Costello, research manager for Museums on the Green at the Falmouth Historical Society, and Amanda Wastrom, curator at the Falmouth Historical Society, were immeasurably helpful and supportive, and for that I'm quite grateful. Antonia Stephens, assistant director at Sturgis Library, and Sturgis' director, Lucy Loomis, were extremely helpful and loaned me beautiful postcards featured in this book.

Bill Cummings, who grew up in Chatham and witnessed the stricken *Pendleton* float by during a storm, provided a fresh and unique look at the greatest small boat rescue in Coast Guard history. I'm thankful for his input, as well as that of Bill's stepdaughter, Linda Apsey.

Historian and author Deborah Hill, founder of North Road Publishing, provided guidance and information about Captain Elijah Cobb of Brewster. Robert Paine Carlson of Eastham and Nancy Viall Shoemaker of West Barnstable are generous historians whose knowledge of Cape Cod graveyards was indispensible. Mary LaBombard, archivist and reference librarian at the W.B. Nickerson Room at Cape Cod Community College, saved the day by generously donating the use of gorgeous photographs that appear in this book. From the Chatham Historical Society, I owe a debt of thanks to Margaret L. Martin and MaryAnn Gray. Desiree Mobed, director of the Harwich Historical Society, was generous as ever with her time and resources.

I'm grateful to my friends Coast Guard Master Chief John E. "Jack" Downey (Ret.) and Captain W. Russell "Russ" Webster (Ret.) for their assistance in the section entitled "A Nor'easter's Familiar Rage, Sea Talk and a Famous Reunion." Emily Eaton and Mark Pokras, DVM, of Tufts University, were very helpful with the essay on loons, as was author and wildlife photographer Heather E. Fone of Centerville. Nina Z. Coleman, Sandy Neck Park manager, and Sean Kortis, turtle monitor at Sandy Neck were equally as helpful with their resources. E.J. Cubellis of Mezza Luna shared his family history in the "Cape Cod's Little Italy" essay, and Meaghan O'Brien provided the photo I used in that essay. My thanks to Emily Eaton, who shared her beautiful image of a loon.

My circle of historian friends was at the ready with advice, including Jim Coogan Jr.; Dick Ryder of Eastham; Duncan Oliver of Yarmouth Port; Barry Homer of Bass River; Fred Dunford, PhD; David Wright of Wellfleet; Bonnie Snow of Orleans; and Phyllis Horton of Dennis Port. Dan Philos-Jensen of Barnstable was the helpful source for the essay on trees.

I'm grateful to the talented crew at The History Press, including acquisitions editor Tabitha Dulla, production editor Darcy Mahan, cover designer Natasha Walsh, publicist Lindsay Lee and independent sales manager Leigh Scott.

And most of all, I reserve my profound thanks to my husband of twenty-six years, Daniel P. Barbo, who has always patiently and with good humor supported my work in historical journalism.

Introduction

What do I mean by the phrase "hidden history"?

Many answers exist according to each person who hears this question and chooses to respond. My own interpretation of what defines hidden history is any nugget in Cape Cod's past that is either brand-new in its public exposure or is retold in a fresh perspective through a story or cited example that's been largely ignored before.

It can be faithfully argued by purists in the field that most—if not all—of Cape Cod's history has already been unearthed, examined, recycled, assessed and written ten times over in the past 250 years.

I agree with this, mostly. Some stories, however, are still untold—either wholly or from a unique angle—and a sampling of those tales is contained in this book.

And it's those stories about which I hope to have a fresh conversation with you, reader. If mainstream history textbooks capture the overall arcs behinds major trends, events, issues or periods in history, writers like myself like to rein in the nuance of ultra-local stories. After all, history isn't always about the major stories of yesteryear or mainline events that have found their way into textbooks. Sometimes a piece of hidden history originates in one village of one town, or in a very small part of Cape Cod, or in a family. It's those kind of stories I want to share with you.

As a writer, I'm always looking or at least hoping for some sort of positive reaction from a reader, even if it's an internal thought of "Oh, I didn't know that." My prime goal is that a reader is educated, enriched, entertained or all of the above and that, to some degree, he or she understands the past through a slightly more enlightened lens. Another goal is that when a reader thinks about the past, it's understood that tales of real human lives are woven into the historical record as one meanders and explores these essays. The craft of writing history is more than fixed dates and events. As a writer, I like to think that history is a dynamic, living, breathing entity—vivid with bright colors, loud noises and movement and the quiet thoughts, bold ideas and voices of people whose laughter and cries are no longer heard. I hope you feel the same way.

Before I started researching and writing this book, I thought I had a pretty good grip on the regional history scene. But I was wrong. I learned a lot and recognized that there is still *much* to learn about Cape Cod's history. I don't think it will ever be a process any one person can accomplish and finish.

Of all the books I have composed, this is the first one in which I have used lengthy and entire passages of what people had to offer, share and say. You'll notice this is very evident in essays entitled "A Nor'easter's Familiar Rage, Sea Talk and a Famous Reunion" and "Off the Rails."

The Hidden History of Cape Cod should not be considered a comprehensive work of every last infinitesimal piece of our neglected past. It would be hugely impossible to fold in twenty volumes of Cape Cod history into a book of this size. That said, this book was assembled to reflect my work as a journalist who has specialized in history for over twenty-five years and who has uncovered a trove of interesting anecdotes and stories about various chapters of Cape Cod history, with a realization and appreciation that there are still many roads and pathways to follow in this field.

Cape Cod's Ancient, Unknown Valley

Remnants of earlier Cape Cod eras are constantly churning in sand not far under our toes.

"If you're in a garden, you might find a nail from 1790 and a stone spear point that's four thousand years old," explained archaeologist Fred Dunford Jr. of Harwich. "Or," he added, "a fragment of a Coke bottle from the 1980s."

Artifacts or things made by people, such as buttons, pottery and an odd coin or two, have been stuck in sands on Cape Cod for dozens, hundreds or thousands of years. Subtle movements of burrowing worms, nesting insects and growing tree root; shifts by a contractor's bulldozer; and the annual freeze-and-thaw processes, to name a few examples, relocate them. Indeed, those spear points, arrowheads, coins, bits of pottery, human and animal bones and many other man-made and natural things aren't actually "layered" into soil in neatly arranged horizontal layers like frozen sediment from the deepest depths of the ocean. These ancient finds migrate and rattle through the soil and below ground, resembling the jumble of a grandmother's kitchen junk drawer. They churn like an ice cream maker at noon in July.

"You can find the glacial bottom" that formed Cape Cod, Dr. Dunford clarified, "but everything above is mixed today."

One of the largest caches of archaeological finds comes from the Stony Brook Valley in modern-day Brewster, which has seen continuous human habitation for over ten thousand years. Other large amounts have also been found around Bass River, Herring River and Wellfleet Harbor, Sandy Neck in Barnstable Harbor and other shorelines where humans settled.

You won't find the Stony Brook Valley on a road map. It's not a destination to which tour guides bring clients. But people live, walk, bike and drive through the valley all the time, and it is another hidden gem rarely written about or discussed on Cape Cod. Stony Brook remains a significant part of the Cape's geologic, cultural and ancient history. "If you could put yourself above the Cape and look down, the Stony Brook Valley begins up at Mill Pond in Brewster, runs downslope out to Cape Cod Bay and drains to the North, which is unusual," Dunford recounts, adding that "other glacial rivers drain to the South," and he's referring to Bass River and Herring River. Apparently, Swan River is the new kid on the geologic block and "doesn't have the same archaeological heritage" as do the other rivers here.

"When the sea level rose, it forced the water table up and formed the valleys," clarified Dunford. Slowly, these waters leveled off and fed the more than one thousand kettle ponds that dot the Cape, and the rivers reverted to tidal waterways. In fact, Bass River is the longest tidal river in the Commonwealth of Massachusetts.

Early native people settled on Cape Cod after walking north and following freshwater river systems slit into the earth by the retreating Laurentian glacier. This glaciation meant that the landscape, Dunford explains, stretched to Martha's Vineyard, Nantucket and south to George's Bank, all of which were connected to Cape Cod.

So the next time you apply sunscreen at Marconi Beach in Wellfleet, or cast a synthetic fishing line off the Bass River Bridge or pedal your bike along the Cape Cod Rail Trail, think about what is swirling in the sand below you: chunks of flint used to build a lifesaving fire, an arrowhead that can still pierce or remnants of a Native American clay pot that once held the food of an Indian grandmother who lived here 150 generations ago.

At this moment, growing tree roots are transporting artifacts and natural remnants of past residents upland in the dirt. Earthworms rope themselves around bits of wood from a centuries-old barn. The spring nudges the soil, which is the gristle of the earth, to awaken and renew itself, and the dirt is on the move, stirring up its ancient secrets. That's what history is: movement and color and seasonal rhythm, people's actions that are long past though their meanings to our culture remain. And when the past is hidden, it's all the more mysterious and thought-provoking.

The ongoing story of Stony Brook Valley is "not information that will change someone's life," reflects Fred, who has studied this region for most of his career, which spans over three decades. "But in the larger scheme of things, people lived here ten thousand years ago."

Get Your Mind in the Gutter

On May 3, 1717, Cyprian Southack sailed to the coast of Wellfleet from Boston to salvage what remained of the one-hundred-foot pirate ship *Whydah*. The British-built merchant vessel was overtaken by pirates and sank in a storm on April 26, 1717, with 143 crewmen. Those killed included its pirate captain, "Black" Sam Bellamy.

Ordered by Massachusetts governor Samuel Shute to retrieve "Money, Bullion, Treasure, Goods and Merchandizes" said to be on the ship, salvage expert Southack had departed for the Cape in short order. To get to Wellfleet from Boston, however, Southack did not sail around the twisted fist of Cape Cod at Provincetown. Rather, his small vessel glided through a secretive, often-hidden and shallow passage that was essentially the first canal that connected Cape Cod Bay to Nantucket Sound. Locals called this waterway "Jeremiah's Gutter," named for Jeremiah Smith, presumably one of the many members of the local Smith family.

For about 150 years, this mile-and-a-half-long waterway saved mariners at least a day in their journey. The Gutter connected Rock Harbor in Orleans to Town Cove in the same town. Orleans historian Bonnie Snow explained that the waterway was the separation line between Eastham and Orleans, and it came in handy during two wars with the British. "Cape Codders would paint their sails red so they wouldn't be seen at night," Snow recounted, while using the Gutter to transport salt, shellfish and salted fish to Boston and New York in exchange for food and supplies during the British blockades in the Revolutionary War and the War of 1812.

This humble waterway was even mentioned by Henry David Thoreau (1817–1862) in Chapter 3 of his iconic book *Cape Cod:*

> *We crossed a brook, not more than fourteen rods long, between Orleans and Eastham, called Jeremiah's Gutter. The Atlantic is said sometimes to meet the Bay here, and isolate the northern part of the Cape. The streams of the Cape are necessarily formed on a minute scale, since there is no room for them to run, without tumbling immediately into the sea; and beside, we found it difficult to run ourselves in that sand, when there was no want of room. Hence, the least channel where water runs, or may run, is important, and is dignified with a name.*

In the early nineteenth century, toward the end of the War of 1812, Jeremiah's Gutter began to close despite being slightly widened in 1804. Eventually, nature took its course. Once Route 6 was under construction, the commonwealth, Snow recounted, "had to build culverts" that further defrayed the remnants of this waterway. What's left of Jeremiah's Gutter—Cape Cod's first canal near the Orleans Rotary and commercial shopping center—is barely noticeable today. But while it existed, it came in handy for locals time and time again.

So what happened on Cyprian Southack's trip to Wellfleet? Not much. He was able to recover only bits and pieces of the treasure, bury a good amount of those who died in the shipwreck and "rescue" two *Whydah* crew members: John Julian, who was part Native American, and a Welshman named Thomas Davis, who later stood trial in Boston.

The small cache of artifacts from the *Whydah* was unearthed by treasure hunter Barry Clifford in July 1998, but the reputed 180 bags of "gold and silver" said to have been stowed in chests aboard the pirate ship remain elusive.

Inside a Cape Cod Home

Henry David Thoreau described Cape Cod houses as being "low and sturdy to the ground, sober looking homes," and how right he was. In other words, practicality took a back seat to pride. The English who settled on the Cape did not have the means or time to show off for their neighbors or construct homes beyond what their funds allowed. As affluence accumulated, pride would outweigh practicality in mere generations.

Architect Sara Porter has often given a lecture entitled "Will the Real Cape Cod House Stand Up?" In it, she says she believes the earlier builders put enormous emphasis on the "economy of materials and function." In other words, "every square inch was used for something."

Many of these old homes have survived—at least, the original bones of these homes have remained. Over time, design elements were incorporated into homes. Between 1700 and 1780, Cape Codders with means started to show off and built colonials in the Georgian style, which came of age during the reigns of four kings named George; these designs, of course, originated in England and drew influence from Italian architecture. The Georgian style emphasized classic details and symmetry, such as a center front entrance.

By 1750, from the Carolinas to Maine, Georgians became all the rage. Cape Codders with deep pockets ordered wallpaper and carpet from Europe, and local tradesmen painted wood paneling—a sign of affluence—in first-floor rooms like parlors. "What your neighbor thought of you was very important," Porter added. This, of course, was years *after* the first white settlers arrived, concerned only with survival. For these settlers, especially women, work was

Above: The Sturgis
Homestead in Barnstable
Village, now the site of the
Sturgis Library, one of the
oldest libraries in the country.
Courtesy of Sturgis Library.

Left: Captain William Sturgis
(1782–1863) was a renowned master
mariner whose voyages to the Pacific
Northwest are well documented. *Courtesy
of Sturgis Library.*

The grocery store and post office of A.H. Bassett in Harwich. *Courtesy of the W.B. Nickerson Archives, Cape Cod Community College.*

endless: nursing children, cleaning, sewing, weaving, spinning, sweeping, mending, gardening, harvesting, dairying, laundering and tending to the chickens, just to name a few of the daily tasks.

Even moderate affluence did not mean that the daily lives of Cape Codders were easy, no matter what type of house they lived in.

On average, each household would burn about eight cords of wood from fall through spring. The fall of 1879 saw a bumper crop of cranberries, but unfortunately, there were too few barrels in which to collect the indigenous fruit. A shortage of fish—especially mackerel and cod—was reported in Cape Cod Bay. Local shops were very busy. The art of retail had claimed Cape Cod, even then. Lumber could be purchased at John Hinckley and Son in Yarmouth Port. In later years, Harry Davidson ran a grocery store near the corner of Route 6A and Wharf Lane at the site of the present-day Just Picked shop, where Christmas Tree Shop used to be. In Yarmouth Port alone, another dry goods store named D.B. Crocker's sold boots and shoes. In October 1879, the *Yarmouth Register* carried an article with helpful household hints for housewives. "Castor oil," the article read, "will soften leather, and corsets with the whalebone removed make good cleaning cloths. A solution of cyanide of potassium is the best poison to kill insects of any kind." And there are others: "Thoroughly wetting the hair once or twice a week with a weak solution of salt water will prevent it from falling out." And "carelessness in changing the underclothing at night accounts for the coarse complexion of many girls."

Few resources were available to young women and ladies of the house other than what they read in the local paper or what their own mothers told them. But in all reality, housekeeping was a serious business, especially in fall. Every Cape Cod home, from the small fisherman's cottages on the banks of Sesuit Harbor in Dennis to the large Greek Revivals overlooking Buzzards Bay in Bourne, had to be outfitted for the coming winter.

By mid-October, a woman would have ordered a barrel each of sugar, flour and salt to see her through to early spring. Ladies harvested apples from local orchards and used them for pies, tarts, cakes, simple snacks and cider. Potatoes and onions were stored in barrels in the buttery or kitchen area. Cucumbers were turned into pickles, and fruits were preserved and stored in the cellar. As the days cooled, the coldest part of the home, the attic, became a seasonal freezer. Hams of slaughtered hogs were cleaned; rubbed with sawdust, salt oats or charcoal; wrapped in cloths; and stored in the attic.

A view of Barnstable Village, circa late nineteenth century, site of the county seat. *Courtesy of Sturgis Library.*

There were socks to darn and mittens to knit, quilts to sew and iron pots to scrub. Within the confines of their own villages, women bartered goods, trading chickens for sugar or potatoes or corn. According to Jane Nylander, author of *Our Own Snug Fireside*, an average New England household was supplied with "pork, corn meal, beef, butter, cheese, molasses, sugar, coffee, tea, spices, corn and other grains."

But what did the average Cape Codder eat every day? Diets were unusually high in saturated fats and low in essential vitamins. Prime sources of protein were highly salted meat and fish.

In 1869, David L. Young of Orleans owned and operated his own boot and shoe retail store "and manufactory" along the county road near Town Cove. In Chatham, Hattie E. Gill opened her millinery store in 1879. And in Bourne, A.R. Eldridge opened a thriving lumber business in 1877 on a wharf on Monument River. All over Cape Cod, hardworking professionals, artisans and tradesmen lived their lives in their own distinctive ways. But one thing that bound these folks was custom and tradition about food.

"Your biggest meal of the day was dinner, which is usually eaten at midday," explained Tom Kelleher, historian and curator at Old Sturbridge Village, which accurately re-creates a nineteenth-century New England village replete with industries, customs and fashions. Dennis historian Phyllis Horton said the biggest meal at midday was timed that way "because they did their hardest work in the daytime. They went to bed early."

"The second biggest meal of the day was breakfast, eaten an hour after rising because you needed time to get the fire started," Kelleher explained. He added the late afternoon or early evening was "tea time," because of the beverage served, and leftovers from the noon dinner were also served then, such as cold meats and cheeses. In the countryside, Kelleher clarified, the afternoon tea was the most social meal. "If you're likely to have company, they are likely to be over for tea."

For generations, "lunch" has become the traditional midday meal. Kelleher explained that lunch or luncheon was "originally a coffee break in mid- to late morning," served about 10:00 or 11:00 a.m., something quick in between breakfast and the noon dinner. When people began working away from their homesteads, they brought their noon dinner with them, and that turned into lunch, which Kelleher said means "a swallow," or a grab-and-go meal. Hence, our current lexicon is now lunch.

Depending on the season, diets varied. A typical breakfast included sausage, ham, eggs and biscuits or johnnycake. The noontime "dinner"—what we call lunch—was the largest meal of the day. If that meal was light, then the evening meal was substantial. The noon dinner began with soup, followed by a main course of either meat or seafood. Cape Codders were serious carnivores: beef, mutton, lamb, chicken or turkey were main entrées that were roasted, boiled, fried or broiled and made into pies, fricassées, hashes or stews.

Organ meats were a real treat and frequently appeared on dinner plates: tripe, liver, tongue, kidneys, hearts or even the whole head. Cape Codders took obvious advantage of seafood with haddock, salmon, shad, mackerel, halibut, trout, herring and even eel served up. Oysters and clams were popular, and lobsters and crabs were turned into salads. Rice, macaroni or sweet potato often appeared, as did a salad in summer followed by a vegetable or two year-round. A dessert of a pudding, a custard, ice cream, a Bavarian cream or a cake was served. If the noon dinner was a huge meal, then only toast with pear sauce, for example, might be on the supper plate.

Compared to today, about the only thing that's different from our diets is the inclusion of a bevy of fresh greens.

In the New England tradition to which most Cape Codders adhered, three meals were eaten. Only when there was a special occasion like a dance or party would Cape Codders consume a large meal in the evening.

Phyllis Horton, eighty-eight, of Dennis Port, remembered, "Every meal had a sweet at the end, called a top-off. My grandfather would say, 'Well, what do we have for top-off?'" The most popular: "Pie," Horton stated.

But some customs never change. In my house, and possibly yours, we still call it Thanksgiving dinner, even if it's served at 1:00 p.m. And the meal's leftovers are still "supper."

The food itself was mostly homegrown until the advent of commercial grocery stores on the Cape past the 1850 mark. Cape Cod was never a wealthy place, unlike some parts of Newport, Boston and other coastal communities connected to the mainland. Kelleher confirmed that Cape Cod was not as prosperous as other parts of Massachusetts. "Old-time Cape Codders lived long lives because they were frugal," Horton explained, adding, "They all had a garden to provide summer and winter food for themselves. They had fruit trees, and grapevines, to 'put by' for the winter. They didn't need cash money. If you needed to feed your family and didn't have a protein," at least in the town of Dennis, "you could go down to the dock and ask a fisherman for a fish to feed your family, and they would never refuse you," she explained.

Local fishermen on the Cape "believed that what God gave to them, they needed to share. And in my time, in Provincetown, that still was a big thing." Phyllis says the Great Depression "did not hit Cape Cod because we were very self-sufficient to begin with. We were poor already. We didn't see a difference."

Boat Landing, Barnstable, Mass.

Cape Codders dropped fishing lines into any waterway, including from this boat landing in Barnstable. *Courtesy of Sturgis Library.*

Still, the average nineteenth-century household was not without proverbial snack food. Special treats included popcorn balls and peanut brittle, orange peel rolled in sugar and just plain oranges.

In the late eighteenth and early to mid-nineteenth centuries on Cape Cod, a woman's day was spent in the keeping room, the central area where life was played out. "Sewing and domestic activities," explained Tom Kelleher, historian and curator at Old Sturbridge Village, took place in the keeping room, and this is where "family kept themselves. On cold winter evenings, a woman caring for children functioned from a keeping room, and this is where she spent most of her retirement."

In the mid- to later days of the nineteenth century, "if you had enough space and had a parlor, like the gentry, you could set aside a room for the 'best parlor.'" This is the room where kids were not allowed. The pastor would visit the family there, and this is where the daughter of the house would marry. The den, or keeping room, what we now call a family room, is where the family would hang out and relax. Before the Victorian era, most Cape Cod homes were less than one thousand square feet, even with a large number of children in the residence.

Everything inside and outside of the house was made of wood: fencing, firewood, furniture and containers like barrels—even vehicles such as wagons and

Portrait of Miss Clara Freeman, a typical young woman coming of age on Cape Cod. *Courtesy of the W.B. Nickerson Archives, Cape Cod Community College.*

sleighs, Kelleher recounted, were made of wood. But the Cape was not totally deforested, unlike what many people think. Yes, it's true you could stand on what is now Route 6A on the Cape's north side and easily see Cape Cod Bay, but "at the height of land-clearing, you still had 'wood lots' of trees" left untouched," he said.

Land was a precious commodity. If today we see only fields, the eighteenth- and nineteenth-century landowners on Cape Cod were much more discerning. If you were a farmer, it would be critical to your livelihood to purchase a tract of land that had both a pasture and a meadow. Another distinction in land transactions included a "dale," an olden English term for a little valley. Differences and distinctions critically mattered then. "Cattle can't graze on a pasture all year long, so you'll need a meadow's grasses to cut for hay," Kelleher said, because meadows are traditionally lowland areas, which can occasionally flood, and those waters feed the grasses farmers will later use for hay. Obviously, today we don't need to care whether land meets the criteria of a meadow or pasture, but in yesteryear on Cape Cod, it was a matter of a landowner's success or failure.

A Burning Grief

The potential of fire to maim and kill was as great as its ability to sustain life.

It may be far from our daily concerns today, but every household on Cape Cod needed fire for warmth, to cook food and to boil water for laundry. If not carefully watched, however, what was a daily necessity was also a constant threat. In modern society, fire is an afterthought, and the hidden concept here is how uppermost fire was in people's minds in past centuries. People feared fire as much as they depended on it for their survival.

On the Cape and throughout New England, cast-iron stoves didn't come into vogue until about 1850. Before that, open-hearth fires were maintained to cook food and for warmth.

A roaring blaze was kept going all day in most New England kitchens, fed with seasoned, dry wood that was neatly stacked nearby. But the same fire that warmed guests on a wintry afternoon could pose a safety hazard that same evening. If not carefully watched over, a stray spark might shoot over to a hearth birch broom and ignite a small fire that would spread like spilled gravy—and quickly. If hot ashes and coals were handled in a careless way, aprons caught fire, as did flammable materials such as flax, bed curtains and dried herbs hanging close by.

Open fires over which huge cast-iron vats of boiling soup or other steaming liquid were hung threatened the safety of children, who spent much of their days in keeping rooms, the modern-day equivalent of a family room. For instance, in March 1826, up in Hennicker, New Hampshire, two siblings

A hearth such as this one appeared in nearly every Cape Cod home. *Courtesy of the W.B. Nickerson Archives, Cape Cod Community College.*

under four years of age were scalded by "the falling of a kettle of boiling soap from a crane." Both soon died of their wounds and were buried in the same coffin.

Dirty chimneys were a source of fires in New England homes. Sparks tumbled down brick chutes, landing in soot, spider webs or perhaps even a dried bird's nest—all fire hazards, indeed.

A Yarmouth man, Richard Keily, received a letter from his brother, Terence, in June 1899 about the death of his five-year-old niece, Annie, who lived in New Zealand. What happened to Annie could have easily occurred to any child living on Cape Cod. "Her mother was washing one day and the little girl was playing in the yard with a little boy when he took her away he had some maches [*sic*] and set fire to some shavings and papers...the wind was blowing very strong at the same time...Annie's clothes caught fire. The little boy ran away. A man heard her screams, and tried to pick up the burning child, but she got two [*sic*] hot for him," Terence wrote, so the man left Annie, alone and on fire, to get some water. When Annie's would-be rescuer returned, the child's skin was burned except for "a band on her neck and waist." Annie was carried home and, in her unquestionable agony, told her astonished mother "what had happened and how the boy took her away and set fire to the shavings." Annie, Terence relayed to Richard, asked only for her favorite hat.

It took Annie three hours to die. She talked up to the time of her death and said she felt no pain. "I just came home from work at half past 5 o'clock while she was telling me how it happened she laid back and died she never cried all the time. I suppose she was too far gone to feel pain she was five years of age."

In our contemporary society, a natural concept of fire is something to which we are not attuned. "It's alien to so many of us," explained Tom Kelleher, historian and curator at Old Sturbridge Village. "We are attuned to auto traffic. We are taught since infancy to 'look both ways.' We have a sense to listen to cars," he noted. Children in Cape Cod homes of yesteryear were always taught to "mind the fire." Over time, most children developed an inherent sense of danger when they were near flames. After all, Kelleher noted, even "in July, food was cooked over an open flame."

A Snapshot of Life on October 25, 1845

When the sun rose on Yarmouth on October 25, 1845, the population of this mid–Cape Cod community was a mere 2,500 people. But for those 2,500 sleepy souls, a long day of work, eating, shopping, school and just plain living was ahead. For a dose of perspective, in 1845, James Polk became the eleventh president of the United States. In 1845, the Oregon Trail was opened, and slavery was still legal in the South. Texas and Florida became states at the time when Yarmouth was already 206 years old. Outside national borders, the first submarine cable was laid across the English Channel, and British engineer William McNaught developed the first compound steam engine.

And Yarmouth, a community coming of age in the mid-nineteenth century, was very engaged as a center of growth and commerce.

James Knowles's General Store in Yarmouth Port had just imported kid gloves from Paris. N.T. Hallet's shop, also in Yarmouth Port, was open for "winter trade," and merchandise included boots, shoes, gloves, shawls, carpeting and hosiery. A handful of retail outlets carried Sherman's Worm Lozengers, which were touted as a treatment to "remove all unpleasant symptoms, and restore to perfect health," according to an advertisement in the *Yarmouth Register and Barnstable County Advertiser.*

Businesses were tucked into the Yarmouth economy from all corners of commerce. A huge rope-making plant measuring roughly eight hundred feet long had been opened in South Yarmouth and was home to a magnesia operation called Fearing and Akin. Numerous saltworks had dotted Yarmouth's coastal borders 170 years earlier, and farms and tiny shops were located in all three villages. The Farris and Judah Baker windmills, along with the Baxter Grist Mill in West Yarmouth, were in full operation. All three villages hosted a post office. South Yarmouth hosted the first one in 1821. The branch in West Yarmouth opened in 1827. Of course, when Yarmouth Port was incorporated as a village in 1829, it, too, had its own post office.

The shoreline was as busy as Main Street. Locals harvested shellfish like bay scallops, soft-shell clams and oysters. Year-round, the boys and men of Yarmouth hunted for geese and ducks along the edge of marshes. Marsh hay itself was a harvestable material that was fed to cattle. Yarmouth has twenty-two kettle ponds—lakes that were carved by glaciers thousands of years ago—and in these waters the boys of Yarmouth lowered their fishing lines to catch pickerel and bass. Two icehouses on Dennis Pond yielded a winter crop of ice that was packed in sawdust and straw and used for lemonade the following summer.

Cape Codders were nothing if not industrious. There were manufacturing industries on the Cape such as ropewalks, factories that turned raw jute into rope used on ships. Once these ropes hit the deck of a vessel, they were known as lines. At any rate, even though we have few factories that make commercial products today, the hidden concept here is that Cape Cod was a mini-factory

An early and successful industry on Cape Cod was brick making, a necessary component to a community's expansion. *Courtesy of Sturgis Library.*

The cultivation of cranberries was a profitable industry on Cape Cod. *Courtesy of Sturgis Library.*

town in its yesteryear days, and the earth provided the raw materials. Brick making, for example, was a thriving industry in West Barnstable.

Cranberry bogs thrived in Harwich, and harvesting salt hay, which made excellent fodder for cattle, took place in nearly every community. Before salt was discovered in upstate New York and there was a railroad to distribute the mineral to market, Cape Codders produced their own harvest from evaporated seawater.

A little-known industry that flourished alongside all maritime-based businesses was anchor dragging. It sounds like a no-brainer and relatively useless, but it was crucial and a good living. For instance, Bass River, which is Massachusetts' longest tidal river and which separates the towns of Dennis and Yarmouth on the south side of Cape Cod, supported fishing boats and sailing packets, not to mention "a variety of ancillary businesses: warehouses, lumberyards and boat yards. Many of these ships lost things overboard, among other things—anchors," wrote Ben Muse Jr. in March 2010 on his fabulous blog. As former anchor dragger Wilfred W. Fuller noted in 1941, anchors were lost in many ways off Bass River and in Vineyard and Nantucket Sounds when boats and larger vessels dropped anchor in storms: "These were lost in various ways. In letting anchors go, the chains would break or unshackle, or the end of the chain would become unfastened. Sometimes in heavy gales the anchors would drag and, to save the vessel from danger of shipwreck, they would slip the chains and thus lose both anchors and chains." Rope attached to two vessels located one-third of a mile apart was "water soaked" until it sank to the bottom, Fuller explained, "with a sixty-pound lead on it near each vessel as a sinker…the anchor fluke or stock would catch the line and stop the vessels." It was an unusual way to make a living, but people made money off this necessary service.

We know the first white Cape Codders farmed. But in the words of one historian, "God performed no miracle on the New England soil. He made the sea. Stark necessity made seamen of would-be planters." So the boys and men of Yarmouth went to sea as whalers, fishermen or merchant mariners. Of the last group, most became sailors, others made first or second mate and the cream of the crop became sea captains. In Yarmouth's maritime history, that one town alone boasted no fewer than several hundred sea captains at any given time during the so-called Great Age of Sail, which was right around 1845.

The lifeblood, of course, of any town on Cape Cod was its people. In 1845, nineteen couples married. The Reverend Nathaniel Cogswell, pastor of Yarmouth's First Congregational Church, conducted most marriage ceremonies. James Gibson, a twenty-five-year-old shoemaker, married Sophia Hallet on October 2. Other men who married in 1845 included a farmer, a mariner, a carriage maker, a physician, a saltmaker, a hat maker, a goldsmith, a merchant and a teamster—a cross-section of society, circa 1845.

Family life flourished. In 1845, sixty-nine babies were born, according to vital statistics located in the vault at Yarmouth Town Hall. And all, of course, were born at home with laboring mothers assisted by their own mothers, sisters, friends, trusted neighbors or midwives. Doctors weren't commonly present at births until much later in the century. Though no children were born in Yarmouth on October 25, 1845, little Maria Eleanor Studley was almost one month old on that day.

On the flip side of life, twenty-three people died in Yarmouth in 1845. Mary Bray was seventy-two when she passed on October 16. On the day Bray died, a baby girl born into the Gage family died within two hours. The cause of death was listed only as "bleeding." But her brief presence lasted long enough for her parents to have named her Clarissa. Yarmouth would lose several more of its youngest and most vulnerable citizens in 1845 to diseases and ailments easily treated today. Cyrus Baker, just ten years old, died of a fever in late October. Just a few weeks earlier, the family of Martha Layman had buried their one-year-old girl, who had succumbed to a "canker rash."

High infant mortality rates were no less common on Cape Cod than in other parts of New England during the 1840s. Nearly one in ten babies died at birth, and one in thirty mothers did not survive labor and delivery. Nearly every family had lost at least one child to disease or illness. Anna Hallet, married for fifty-nine years to Captain Bangs Hallet, lost seven of their nine children between 1837 and 1846, including an unnamed infant who died in 1845.

If babies in the earlier decades of the nineteenth century survived their births, it was often the food that made them sick or even killed them. We must assume that some mothers across Cape Cod also followed what was common practice in New England communities at the time: attempting to feed infants food fit only for older children and adults. Medical logic of the time dictated that newborns be fed a dab of butter with sugar, softened bread with pork and catnip tea with a drop of gin. Beer, milk, biscuits and meat were also force-fed to infants—not always but often. Is it any wonder, then, that intestinal diseases were a chief cause of death among infants in the early decades of the 1800s? It was only later in the nineteenth century that doctors stumbled on the fact that babies who were breastfed by their mothers seemed to live longer than other newborns.

Children enrolled in Yarmouth's public schools studied from the District School Reader, a book series in use in Boston, Worcester and elsewhere in Massachusetts. When they weren't in school, boys swam and fished in warm weather, and in winter they skated and sledded. Girls played with rag dolls, and those from wealthier families perhaps received real dolls, those with glass eyes and real hair.

Indentured and Served

On April 5, 1840, the young life of James B. Lord, fourteen, would be altered forever. That's the day his father, Rand, signed his son over to a farmer identified simply as "C. Swift" of Falmouth. James was to become Swift's indentured servant.

The contract, provided by the Falmouth Historical Society, noted that James was to "learn the art, trade and mystery of farming [and] that [C.S. Swift] will also cause the said minor to be suitably instructed in reading, writing, arithmetic, &c. by causing him to attend the public school or schools, kept as required by the laws of this commonwealth, 12 weeks at least in every year till he shall have attained the age of eighteen years."

It is assumed that James was from the Boston area since the indenture document used as a template was from the Boston Asylum and Farm School for Indigent Boys.

Farmer Swift, per this contract, had agreed to "train him up in the habits of industry, sobriety and virtue…[and] provide and allow the said minor during the said term, wholesome and sufficient meat, drink, lodging, clothing, and all other things, in health and sickness, necessary and suitable for his situation and employment."

The process of indenture was viewed as a worthy salvation for families of limited means. In exchange for providing a public school education, food and board, a farmer or skilled craftsman would take in an indentured servant, or apprentice, under a contract anywhere from four to seven years or until that servant turned the legal age of twenty-one. In James Lord's case, he would be indentured until February 19, 1847, his twenty-first birthday.

If Swift failed to live up to the terms of his contract, Rand Lord had the option of reclaiming James "and to bind him out to any other person for the residue of the said term, anything in this indenture to the contrary notwithstanding." In other words, if James had, say, three years left on his contract, his father had the option of signing over James to someone else for those three years.

In the nineteenth century, up to two-thirds of white people who immigrated to the American colonies up to the time of the American Revolution were indentured servants in the lower U.S. colonies in exchange for their passage from Europe, and these individuals were sought after by retailers and farmers.

It's impossible to know how many humans arrived on Cape Cod from other parts of Massachusetts or elsewhere as indentured servants, but they were indeed part of the nineteenth-century workforce here, a hidden fact of regional history. This topic has received limited attention, perhaps because more important events and historical trends rated a higher grade of scholarly attention than "mere" domestic matters.

But as I compose this, I wonder what had happened to James. What kind of life did he have after he left the Swift farm? One thing is for certain. When he turned twenty-one, under the terms of the indenture contract his father signed with C. Swift, James was to have been given "two suits of clothes, complete, and suitable to his degree and standing in life, and one hundred dollars in cash." Clearly and unfortunately, some aspects of Cape Cod's history may lie hidden forever.

As harsh as it sounds to us to be one, indentured servants played an important part in the labor workforce. If treated well, these individuals received on-the-job training and skills for their future lives.

Upper-class Cape Cod households employed multiple servants. Indentured servants were under the auspices of only the middle class: farmers, artisans and tradesmen. In the later years of the nineteenth century, higher-income families constructed huge mansions and brought their servants with them when they summered on the Cape. These employees were of an entirely different grade than indentured servants.

James Madison Beebe was a dry goods magnate from Boston, and in 1866, Eben Jordan, founder of the famed Jordan Marsh retail franchise, bought his business. This coincided with Beebe's discovery that Cape Cod, a short train ride from Boston, was indeed the place to summer, albeit a

Daniel Mascarello was employed as a butler by the Beebe family of Falmouth. *Purchased from the Falmouth Historical Society.*

Four servant girls employed by the Beebe family in Falmouth enjoy a rare excursion at the beach. *Purchased from the Falmouth Historical Society.*

lesser-known enclave than snobby Newport. "In 1872, Beebe bought the Thomas Swift House on Shore Street with surrounding acreage, and in the following year he purchased 95.5 acres of high ground above the railroad station from J.S. Fay," wrote the Reverend T.E. Adams Jr. in the winter 1989 edition of *Spritsail,* a biannual journal published by the Woods Hole Historical Collection.

With a family so wealthy, there is no doubt the household included at least a dozen servants, including a chauffer, a gardener, maids, a cook and kitchen helpers and a head housekeeper. Of course, the family also had a butler, Daniel Mascarello, who oversaw the entire household.

James Beebe passed on in 1875. Survivors included two sons, Pierson Beebe, and his brother, James Arthur Beebe. "His children created a hundred acre farm on Shore Street, and built Waterside in 1876 overlooking Vineyard Sound. They also built two English style manor houses on the high ground: Highfield Hall in 1878 in half-timber motif, and the Anglo-Dutch style Tanglewood in 1879," recounted Reverend Adams. Pierson owned Highfield Hall, and James Arthur was master at Tanglewood.

Botanical Sentinels

They hide in plain sight and line our streets like silent sentinels, perfectly spaced apart. Decades ago, someone thought to plant the same species of tree in a row like living icons to land conservation or outside botanical art. We might ask ourselves how much we notice these indispensible elements of our native landscape. We drive our cars, ride our bikes and walk by the tangible evidence of someone long dead who felt that trees were to be cherished.

"Trees complete the landscape. They cast shadows and dappled light that remind us to look up once in a while to appreciate nature and our surroundings," explained Dan Philos-Jensen of Barnstable, a landscaper who studied landscape architecture and forestry at the University of Massachusetts–Amherst. "They are living beings, and no two are alike. They are purposeful and balanced, and each cell nurtures all living things in a grand, miraculous ecosystem," he added, calling trees "the eternal guardians of the earth."

Some years ago I started to notice patches of these vertical sentinels along Route 6A, the most northerly thoroughfare on Cape Cod. From then on, I had always wondered who might have planted them and why. Sometimes I imagined a farmer or homeowner from the mid-nineteenth or early twentieth century putting on a pair of work boots and then measuring by foot the distance between each young tree.

If these trees were lining a walkway or path, they would be considered an allée, a French landscape term. But along a roadway or street, they are merely the fancy of a nature lover who lived a long time ago and appreciated a botanical urban landscape.

A perfectly aligned row of trees along Strawberry Lane in Yarmouth Port. *Courtesy of Theresa M. Barbo.*

An English weeping beech, imported from England in the nineteenth century, adorns a private lawn in SandySide, Yarmouth Port. *Courtesy of Theresa M. Barbo.*

When the English permanently settled on Cape Cod, their first days were spent exploring native forests that were "all wooded with oaks, pines, sassafras, juniper, birch, holly, vines, some ash, walnut; the wood for the most part open and without underwood, fit either to go or ride in," according to the seminal book *Mourt's Relation*. Clearly, the wood here was bountiful and beautiful. But within one hundred years, these native woodlands were no more except for planned wood lots. Hosting wood lots was the extent of forestry management by colonists. Native Americans employed an ancient slash-and-burn agricultural method to clear a forest to raise crops. Today, we see the woodlands for their beauty, but in yesteryear, native trees served a utilitarian purpose.

Wood equaled survival. Trees were cut and used for furniture, fencing, boats and ships, flooring, actual houses and, most importantly, firewood. The average Cape Cod home burned eight cords of firewood from early fall through spring. A full cord of 128 cubic feet measures four feet high, four feet wide and eight feet long. And there was only so much wood one could scrape out from an island. By the early 1800s, you could stand in my home village of Yarmouth Port on Main Street, today's Route 6A, and look north and see the waters of Cape Cod Bay; that's how clear-cut the trees were.

Clear-cutting land, such as the clearing for a large shopping center, Dan says, "voids the land of a very important root mass. So many symbiotic relationships in the soil balance out the ecosystem in that particular environment." Lopping down trees rids the landscape of texture, he says, and "limits the landscape to just being a ground cover, varying from zero to five feet tall."

And maybe that's why people started to think differently about their landscape and actually thought to start planting again. What's that old Greek proverb? "A society grows great when old men plant trees whose shade they know they shall never sit in."

These trees, perfectly aligned with their canopies nodding to one another, are in plain sight for all to see. The next time you're driving, biking or walking along 6A, and without distracting yourself too much, look at the trees and see if you notice the living dreams and work of conservation of a municipal ancestor. Looking at them reminds me of a classic work of fiction, *The Man Who Planted Trees* by Jean Giono.

Our landscape has not been the same aesthetically since the 1960s, when Dutch elm disease felled an army of American elms that had been planted a century earlier, but there remains beautiful trees that shade us in return for our appreciation of them.

The Character of Wellfleet

If it's true that no two children in the same family are alike, and personalities differ in clans, the same can be said for each of Cape Cod's fifteen towns. Often a hidden concept in this iconic place, each municipality has its own personality, even though we share the same sands, shores and woodlands.

The one common denominator, perhaps, and especially in yesteryear, was a sense of independence. Just as members of the "eastern parish" of Yarmouth broke off to establish the Town of Dennis in June 1793, and the "north parish" of Harwich untied the apron strings to incorporate into the Town of Brewster in 1803, Wellfleet shed its formal ties to Eastham and established itself as its own entity in May 1763.

All that said, from the get-go, Wellfleet was the Outer Cape's "frontier town," according to Wellfleet historian David Wright, author of *The Famous Beds of Wellfleet: A Shellfishing History.* Wright says that Wellfleetians have been "proud, resourceful, difficult to rule, in every decade in our 250-year-old history."

From the moment Captain Myles Standish led an exploration party from the *Mayflower* onto land inhabited by the Pononakanet tribe, Wellfleet has been what Wright calls a "remote, hardscrabble place." On the other hand, Wellfleet's fierce independence has served it well. Its residents "weren't farmers until they had to eat," Wright recounts, and they "weren't fishermen until the topsoil blew away." Native Americans showed early residents how to shore-whale, or harvest dead whales. Soon, Wellfleetians took to the sea, and Wright notes, "In 1765, 420 men were sailing out of the Wellfleet

Harbor on twenty to thirty ships heading for Davis Straights and the coast of Africa" for whales.

In truth, the residents of Wellfleet have hung on to their independence by brilliantly adapting to commercial trends. They became traders and transporters, fishermen, merchant mariners and sea captains. "What has stayed the same through the centuries and even today keeps the town's identity intact is the natural presence and cultivation of shellfish," Wright states. Indeed, he adds that Wellfleet has "supplied more oysters than any other town in New England."

Captain Lorenzo Dow Baker brought home to Wellfleet a shipment of green bananas from Jamaica in 1870. After the bananas turned yellow and tasted great, Captain Baker introduced a new industry to the United States—the import of bananas through commercial markets—and expanded his fleet to accommodate this new industry. And by 1885, the Boston Fruit Company was offering public stock. Later, the United Fruit Company that was formed in 1899 became the Chiquita brand.

Additionally, a hotel Captain Baker owned and named the Chequesset Inn, which employed Jamaicans, kicked off the movement of Wellfleet as a summer tourist destination.

Perhaps it's the lack of elbowroom that makes Wellfleet unique. At its narrowest point, the town is three miles wide. But Wright explains that the town itself hosts two dichotomies: a very calm Cape Cod Bay to Wellfleet's west and the "roaring Atlantic" to the east, not to mention "all those kettle ponds and forests in between."

"Economically, Wellfleet has changed," explains Wright, "but the irascibility remains."

Chatham's Last Sea Captain

One late summer afternoon in 1853, in a weathered farmhouse close to today's Chatham Bars Inn, twelve-year-old Sammy Harding politely but gravely told his widowed mother that he was going to sea, and that was that.

A son of a sailor, the lad—small for his age, but sturdy in spirit—never looked back, and he signed on as a cabin boy aboard the *Rose Poole* from Boston. "I got six dollars a month and a licking a day," he would later recount to author Katharine Crosby. "It's the easiest way to learn because you don't have to be told twice."

Sammy was one of thousands of young Cape Cod boys who went to sea during the eighteenth and nineteenth centuries, working as cabin boys, valets to captains and galley assistants. If these boys passed muster, they "went aloft," becoming sailors who earned twelve dollars a month. Sammy did well his first year at sea. At thirteen, he visited Chatham with nearly eighty dollars in cold hard cash, a fortune then, for his Mum.

The work was physically demanding, and rules were learned hard and fast. How to manage rigging, coil lines and tie knots. Climb the masts, and stand against the wind. Grease the masts. Mend the sails. And most important of all, don't ever look down.

For young boys like Sammy, injuries and wounds were common at sea. What sailor did not suffer at least a rope abrasion from hauling lines? A toothache, a broken finger here or there and the dreaded scurvy, a vitamin deficiency disease that turned skin into Play-doh and swelled the gums so badly you couldn't open your mouth. A fall from high up a mast could snap a neck like dry kindling.

But that was a quicker, kinder death than tumbling into the ocean, which is what happened to one nameless Cape Cod sailor on July 18, 1868, when he fell from the bowsprit of the *Rival* into heavy seas off the southern African coast.

The captain's wife, Mrs. Didama Kelley Doane of West Harwich, recorded the tragedy in her famous diary: "The ship was going nine knots at the time and must have passed right over him. The mate says he saw him once just astern and threw him the grating, but he was a clumsy fellow and could not swim, and having a good many clothes on, [I] suppose he soon sank."

You could bet a day's worth of hardtack that the sailor wasn't dead before his trunk was rifled through, and his personal belongings were then divided among shipmates who quickly offered up a sailor's prayer for his soul, all the while pocketing his knife and stowing his oilskins. Efficient, sea life was.

Still, the journey had its fun. Abundant natural wonders unknown to land boys and men were commonplace sights at sea. Waterspouts closing in on a ship. Dolphins piercing the waves that bounced off the ship in the South Pacific. The exotic taste of fresh coconut milk as it dribbled down the side of a sailor's mouth on shore leave in Hawaii. And lucky was the sailor on friendly terms with the cook, whose repertoire ranged from fresh chicken to pork and beans to "bread," which was only flour and water in most cases.

Saltier tales abound about a sailor's shore leave. One night at a brothel in a busy port city could cost a sailor his monthly wages if he foolishly wagered them. Drunk, he stood the chance of being kidnapped by a crew-thirsty captain from another vessel, only to wake the next morning on another ship under the command of a new captain.

Cape Cod gave up its boys and men to the sea willingly, generation after generation. As for why, the great maritime historian Samuel Eliot Morison said it best: "Tradition, love of adventure, desire to see the world and the social prestige of the shipmaster's calling were partly responsible for Yankee boys going to sea. Few could grow up in a seaport town and resist the lure."

Before railroad and steam barges, tall ships were the only way to get people and goods between continents. From England came candles, shoe leather, axes and furniture. The British needed whale oil, and they loved our New England timber, which burned brighter and better than peat moss. Teas, silks, firecrackers and spices from China left port at Canton, bound for London. In London, porcelain china and iron goods were taken to Boston, and from there, for example, barrels of molasses and numerous New England exports were taken all over the world.

Captain Samuel G. Harding is considered Chatham's last great sea captain. *Courtesy of the Chatham Historical Society.*

Cape Cod sea captains and their crews were world-renowned for their expertise, dependability and endurance. Master mariners got all the glory, but it was the sailors who were the muscle and machine of any vessel, be it large or small. With few deep-water harbors, Cape Cod could not host the lucrative and larger ships that required deep drafts. But by offering its boys and men to the merchant marine, the Cape remained competitive in global maritime trade.

The world was a big, watery highway, especially during the Great Age of Sail in the mid-nineteenth century. One intersection between the longitude of twenty-eight degrees and thirty degrees west on the equator supposedly drew winds said to be the strongest, a prime route frequented by tall ships, much like Route 6 is for cars on a summer Sunday. "I counted twenty-four sails in sight," said one sailor who remembered crossing the equator, "making out one ship, thirteen barks, one barkentine, two full-rigged brigs, three brigantines, one schooner and three others too far away to be identified."

By sixteen, aboard the *Seabird*, young Sammy was a second mate, and at the age of twenty-two, people addressed him as Captain Samuel G. Harding, Chatham's last deep blue–water man.

In his later years, Captain Harding was described as a "fine, upstanding old gentleman with a ruddy face and snowy sideburns and mustache." Captain Harding was, at eighty-five, known to have worn a heavy gold watch that dangled from his black vest and probably reflected off his shiny black shoes. In his last years, he was all vigor and dignity and no-nonsense. That's indeed quite different from his experience as a cabin boy of twelve when he saw the frigate *Constitution* through a porthole of his first ship off the west coast of Africa. "Oh, gorry," he gushed to the captain, whose dinner he almost spilled. "Gorry, ain't she BIG? Ain't she a BEAUTY?!"

Life, Completed

Author's note: There's something about a diary that's magical and intriguing at the same time—and perhaps tinged with a bit of voyeurism. But by peeking into the mind, heart and soul of someone dead long ago, we gain a perspective into a segment of history that no textbook or newspaper of the day can capture: a true sense and human feeling of bygone eras.

In the nineteenth century, recording one's thoughts, experiences and opinions was commonplace, but over the years many of these original pieces of humanity have been lost, thrown out or are unreadable. How many stories will forever remain hidden because these chronicles of the human experience have been lost?

Many years ago, I found a white plastic bag in a file somewhere at the Yarmouth Port Library. Inside were five or six slim diaries composed by Stephen Sears of South Yarmouth, a solid citizen who recorded his feelings on papers; it's my hope that readers will find his unique narrative interesting.

The only thing left is his words, which breathe today as a testament to a seasoned life of loss, love and meaning. Between 1875 and 1905, Stephen Sears of South Yarmouth, a teacher and civic leader, poured his soul into nine diaries—of which only a handful survive—yet they yield an album of emotion, civic duty, hard work and meaning from his days as a selectman, Sunday school teacher, bookseller, father, husband, brother and neighbor. "Good morning, my promised companion of the coming year; now let us be friends, true friends, confiding and trusting; as I familiarly commit to you the secrets of my life so will you as youthfully preserve them,"

Sears wrote on January 1, 1883. The handwriting is beautiful, scripted in classic black ink by a person who was clearly well educated.

Nature entries litter passages here and there, usually tucked in between work notes. In early 1883, on January 4, Sears wrote, "The past comes up with the freshness of youth. The river [we presume Bass River] the salt-marshes, the woods, the plains, all resound with the tale of boyhoods' sports and remind me so forcibly of the companionship of my father with whom my tired but willing feet cheerfully followed and to whom my growing hands were ever obedient [sic]." Four days later, Sears remembered, "Three years to [the] day since Mother died."

On January 16, Sears "spent most of the time in making ready for school… Took the keys of the school house," where he spent "six hours in the school room." Clearly humble, Sears wrote, "Never do I feel as small as when I stand before a school in the capacity of a teacher."

The mundane rudiments of daily life in the late nineteenth century are faithfully detailed, and those include the "oiling and cleaning [of] a harness," and another day Sears "made [a] towel roller and ground axes this forenoon." Sears always mentioned the barn he was building. During January, Sears kept himself busy "clearing nails from the old barrels that were donated for my prospective barn."

As a teacher and later a selectmen in the town of Yarmouth, Sears was engaged in civic affairs from tax assessments to finances to planning to caring for the poor. "We were at the almshouse.

STEPHEN SEARS
EIGHTH GENERATION
B. JULY 15, 1822
D. DECEMBER 26, 1907 SO. YARMOUTH. MASS.

Stephen Sears's diaries provide a front-row seat to Yarmouth's history. *Purchased from the Historical Society of Old Yarmouth.*

Had business for the entire day," wrote Sears on June 12, 1883. "Solomon the pauper died last night, making the third male pauper in a few weeks." On June 21, 1883, Sears "finished up valuation of the north side," and on June 26 Sears said he was "early at our assessors' work. Applied ourselves closely all day."

And so his life went.

"Went to call Dr. Sears to Mrs. Oliver, who made an attempt at suicide this morning," he wrote on June 16, 1891. His son, Dr. Sears, was the physician about whom he wrote.

Stephen was born in July 1822 and was a son of Barnabus Sears and a direct descendant of Richard Sears, one of the first white settlers who arrived in Mattacheese, later renamed Yarmouth, in 1640. Stephen lived his entire life in Yarmouth as a true son of Bass River.

The 1893 diary was mostly a reflection of routine activity, but it's still very interesting. On January 5, 1893, Sears wrote, "A long cheerful evening gives us time for reading our weeklies." On May 5, Sears reflected, "Nothing worthy of note this morning. This afternoon I attended Bangs Hallett's funeral…" Bangs Hallett was an important figure in town. Though his last years were lived at his daughter's home in Fairhaven, Captain Bangs Hallett and his late wife, Anna, were both Yarmouth born and raised their family in that mid-Cape town. Anna would predecease him, as would eight of their nine children, most of whom died in infancy or as toddlers. Bangs was a sea captain in the China trade and sailed from Boston to the Far East dozens of times.

Sears was seventy-one in 1893 but remained very active in community affairs, vitally dedicated to his work as a Sunday school teacher. On January 17, Sears asked a rhetorical question in his diary: "Why am I so interested in this S'.S'. work? Because I think it is the best thing I can do for the coming generation."

A truly hands-on man, much of the upkeep on Sears's home he handled himself. Month by month, the yellowing, fragile pages of his dairy reveal snippets of domestic history that come to life in a reader's imagination, and quite clearly, too. Sears wrote that he "painted the chamber set 3rd coat" or "ploughed garden and planted peas" and "hauled home a cord of wood." In fact, Sears made many references to tending the earth because nearly every house had a kitchen garden. But the hard physical work took a toll on him just the same. "I do not know what the harvest shall yield but the labors are abundant," he composed in his diary in late May 1893. On June 2, Sears "built a cage around a tree and burnt caterpillars." On June 6,

Sears declared that "summer is here, hot and dry," and later that day he "transplanted tomato vines and hoed my watermelons."

Every day Sears watered the garden and sometimes fed the soil seaweed, a natural fertilizer. After three weeks of no precipitation, a welcome rainstorm on June 17 inspired Sears to write, "The ground is wet again and vegetation smiles." June 21 was a long diary entry because Sears took a trip to what we now know as Great Island in West Yarmouth, where he checked out a proposed roadway by the island's owner, a "Mr. Cory." Sears also noted that Lizzie Borden was found "not guilty" in the axe murders of her father and stepmother, a verdict that he noted "gives us joy." Plus, "new potatoes appear [on] our table at dinner."

By the middle of June, Sears "rejoices in an increasing crop," but toward the end of that month, he writes, "If I were to offer sacrifice to the Devil it should be potato bugs in Lager Beer." In early July, Sears recorded the "first cucumbers today." And in August, his garden yielded "potatoes, berries, squashes, cucumbers and corn."

For a spell that summer, Sears must have worked as a teacher during the week at a private school in Providence and then come home weekends because in June 1893 he also wrote, "Mrs. Palmer is dissatisfied with six dollars per week for my board. She thinks her room is worth more, so I pay her the 7-dollars but think it too much." Apparently arguing over a dollar was not worth Sears's time or dignity.

The summer of 1893 was ending, and preparations for fall began. On August 17, Sears "carted two and a half tons of coal for Barnabus [his brother] and hauled home a cord of wood for myself."

In early September, Sears planted the fall "bedding crop" and "shelled beans and plucked the first watermelons."

Three years later, Stephen Sears and his beloved wife, Henrietta "Ett" Sears, celebrated their golden wedding anniversary on April 16, 1896. "Fifty years of wedded bliss. Today we call on friends, relatives and neighbors to rejoice with us upon this festive occasion. A goodly number is with us this afternoon and evening. Presents unexpected but as follows: gold-$63.50, greenbacks, 16."

Sears always followed community news, whether it was joyous or tragic. On Sunday, July 12, 1896, he wrote, "William Eldridge drowned this forenoon…in Bass River…He went fishing and by means unknown fell overboard and was left to meet the result of his folly. His body was found about 4:00, near the mouth of the river. His watch stopped at 9-thirty. Untimely indeed." Years later, of a friend's passing on January 25, 1905,

Sears would write, "John C. to be laid away at 2-pm. Nature frowns upon the departure of one so worthy of life."

One of the last entries that I could find was in 1905. Sears's handwriting was not steady as it had been in earlier years. On December 31, Sears composed, "April weather continues to the surprise of all. How favorable for such who have small supplies of fuel." Ever witty, ever caring.

Stephen Sears died on December 26, 1907, and is buried alongside Henrietta in the Baptist Cemetery on Old Main Street near his beloved Bass River.

Captain America

In our contemporary lexicon, the phrase "the Greatest Generation" refers to those coming of age during World War II and the veterans of the European and Pacific Theatres of War who saved the world from the Germans and Japanese. Hidden to most of the world are the impact of eighteenth- and nineteenth-century American merchant mariners and their immersion in global marketplaces that significantly advanced the American economy, immigration patterns and maritime diplomacy, beginning just after the Revolution.

Before the advent of steam travel, the world's commercial goods were transported between continents by tall ships in the 1700s and 1800s. A majority of those sea captains were American, and most of those American skippers hailed from New England—Cape Cod, specifically. In Dennis, for example, 371 sea captains called that small town home. In West Dennis alone, that village boasted 124, and "the populations of these villages weren't very big," according to historian Phyllis Horton. "Almost every man in Dennis was a sea captain."

What you're about to read is an essay on one of Cape Cod's sea captains from the "pioneering" days at sea, Elijah Cobb of Brewster. He composed a diary, and its content reveals an example of bravery, vision and character that was commonplace in yesteryear. Accomplished at young ages, these captains sailed the world bearing the United States flag. They put themselves in dangerous situations and were exposed to strange cultures and circumstances that were often deadly, all on behalf of commerce and country, bearing witness to famous political and historic events in history. Captain Cobb, for example, was in the midst of the French Revolution. Here is a hidden slice of Cape Cod, with some dialogue in Cobb's own words.

His was a life beautifully littered in meaning and accomplishment, and he was a devoted husband with a loving wife, children and grandchildren. So, at the ripe age of seventy-five, Captain Elijah Cobb (1768–1818) began to record his life story "for the Gratification and amusement of my beloved Grand-Children."

And Captain Cobb did not sugarcoat his humble beginnings. Elijah was one of six children and a son of a sea captain himself. But his father's untimely death at the age of thirty-three when sailing from Cadiz, Spain, to Quebec left his widowed mother impoverished with a farm to run, including a small house and barn on their homestead. Normally in these circumstances, the owner of a vessel will provide some sort of death benefit to widows, and Mrs. Cobb, wrote Elijah, was expecting at least $100 "for my Father's effects," but the cash never arrived. With little recourse, Mrs. Cobb distributed most of her children to other people to help raise. "Some of us must leave the perternal dwelling & seek subsistence among strangers," Cobb recounted. "My Bro, being the Elder, was tried first, but wou'd not stay, & came home crying. I was then in my 6th year, & although too young to earn my living, I left my dear mother for that subsistence among strangers which she could not procure for me." It can be assumed that young Cobb was indentured in some way to strangers because he later remembered, "I continued from my Mother except at times visiting her until in my 13th year, when by an imprudent attempt to lift beyond my strength, I broke a vessell in my stomack, which entirely disenabled me" sometime during 1782. "I was sent home, incapable of labour of any kind."

For one year, young Elijah was home with his cherished mother, who nursed her son back to health. The family doctor suggested the lad "be sent to sea as the best method to regain my health."

In the fall of 1783, Cobb was "fitted out" for Boston, and this was the usual pathway for Cape Cod boys and young men. Up to this time, Cobb was not doing anything out of the ordinary. As historian Henry Kittredge noted, Cape Cod was known as the "greatest nursery of seamen in North America." Most of the master mariners traversing global routes were Americans, with most from New England and even a greater number from Cape Cod. The reason the Cape wasn't a major maritime commercial market was because it didn't have a harbor deep enough for a brig, which is roughly eighty tons, with the exceptions of Provincetown and Woods Hole Harbors. (Just ask the British.) "Brigs were used for all commerce and had been for quite a while," explained historian Deborah Hill, who edited the second edition of Cobb's diaries. (The first Cobb diary was published in 1925 by Yale University Press.)

So off Cobb went to see the wide world when he had never even been off Cape Cod. Indeed, even Boston must have been a great shock to him in 1783. "My whole wardrobe was packed in a gin case for a trunk; a tow bed-sack, filled with rye straw, & a pair of home made blankets for sleeping appuratis, with two bushels of corn to pay my passage to Boston—and acquipted thus, I left the family circle, with buoyant sperits, and in full confidence that I should work myself thro life, with honour & credit." (Corn was often used as currency, especially for a family with few resources, which explains why he brought bushels of corn for his trip to Boston.)

Cobb didn't travel by stagecoach because that mode of transport didn't exist then. His options were to walk or go by horse or sea. He was booked on a water taxi or packet boat, which traveled a fixed route and timetable between Cape Cod and Boston. They were usually on time, except when they weren't, disabled by a lack of wind that didn't fill the sails or too much wind, which idled the vessels during storms. And when Cobb boarded the *Creture*, a twenty-five-ton schooner at Skaket, they sailed to Provincetown but were forced to retreat to a safe harbor there for nearly three days during a gale. (There's a chance, given Elijah's poor spelling, that the schooner was not named *Creture*, but rather, *Creature*.)

When he arrived in Boston, poor Elijah soon learned that the supply of earnest seamen outweighed the demand to fill berths. "Frequently the best of seamen were destitute of voyages," he recalled. "Several of our neighbouring young men had been to Boston that fall, previous to my leaving home, & had returned without giting employ." Indeed, friends told Mrs. Cobb she would be foolish to "spend" corn on Elijah thinking he would just waste it, but she had faith in her boy, and this faith was not misplaced. The first time Elijah hit the docks "and stood gazing at a new vessel, wondering, & admiring her monstrous size, her great cables & anchors &c, a gentleman stept from her deck & thus accosted me."

That gentleman turned out to be the captain.

"My lad, do you want a voyage?"

"Yes, sir!"

"Will you go with me in this vessel?"

"Where are you bound, sir?"

"To Siranam [Surinam, as noted by Hill at the end of this piece]."

After some back and forth, the pair agreed to terms. As a cabin boy, Elijah would earn half a sailor's wages, about $3.50 per month, or $32.00 in today's currency. Still, it was a lot for a boy who had traveled to Boston with only two bushels of corn. Hearing that the captain had no first mate, Elijah promised to return the next morning with one: his uncle. "I then wrote to Mother that I had got a voyage for myself & Uncle, & if those young men would come to Boston before I sailed, I would ship them off, too, rather than have them stay at home Idle all winter."

The voyage went well, except for a bout of seasickness, which was to be expected. Elijah "found I was able to give pretty good satisfaction in my line of duty. My particular attention to the officers procured me some presents, by which I was enabled to purchase a Barrel of molasses & some fruit for an adventure back to Boston."

In the spring of 1784, Elijah Cobb disembarked from the vessel in Boston and was paid twenty-one dollars. He also sold the barrel of "molases & some of my fruit," and used the money to "git myself a new suit of sailors cloaths from the Slopshop, & carried home & put in my Mothers hand, 20 silver Dollars—probably the largest sum of money she had possesd since she had been a widow, & that from her poor little sick Boy."

Diaries contain remembrances, of course, and personal facts, like birth dates. But hidden are the memories of pure emotion, which is why the recounting of Cobb's diary is so important in our time. "Her tears flowed freely upon the occasion, but they were tears of gratitude to our heavenly Father, for his mercies to her child in permitting his return home in so much better health than he left it." And hidden until his diary surfaced was Cobb's devotion to this mother. In Cobb's brief recounting of his life, we see the gristle and grit of hardship of his time that is simply not found in any textbook.

After a short time at home, Cobb spent the next several years aboard a coastal schooner and then shipped off as a "common sailor," traveling several times back and forth to India. Clearly, our Elijah had gotten his sea legs. There was never a question now that Cobb would ever farm or take up a land trade; the sea was his new office and workplace.

Once he returned from his latest overseas voyage in December 1786, Cobb learned that his brother had fallen from the mast of a ship in Delaware Bay. This unnamed brother had broken both legs, one of which had to be amputated. He had also injured a thighbone and sustained serious shoulder injuries. Winter prevented Elijah from visiting until the spring of 1787. That's when Cobb walked to Boston with three other sailors, "joined the vessell, loaded her, & saild for Philadelphia." Cobb finally was able to see his brother. A month later, in the same year, his brother was well enough to visit Cape Cod and travel "home to our Mother."

For at least another year, Cobb continued to work for his senior relatives at Benjamin Cobb & Sons of Boston. By this time, he had been promoted to mate and served under "many different captains" for the next six or seven years.

It was then that Cobb felt he was qualified to captain a vessel himself. But for some unknown reason, Cobb's relatives did not hire him out as a captain, so he left for Baltimore, where he made two voyages to Europe as a first mate. Finally, after Cobb returned to Boston and assumed command of a brig "in the employ of Edwd & William Reynolds," he had made the rank of captain, just like his father, and assumed a new hierarchy in society. "After making several voyages to Virginia & one to the West Indies, I went to the cape in April, 1793, and got married. I was then in my 25th year."

The Virginia trade occupied Captain Cobb for the next two years before the Messrs. Reynolds sent him to Europe aboard the brig *Jane*. To avoid Moslem pirates in the Mediterranean—mariners Cobb called "algerines," who extorted protection money from Americans—Cobb sailed for Curruna in northern Spain instead of his original destination of Cadiz. But Cobb could not avoid trouble, and the crew of a French Frigate "capturd & sent me to France, & here commenced my first trouble & anxiety as a ship Master, having under my charge a valuable vessel & cargo, inexperienced in business—carried into a foreign port, and unacquainted with the language, no American consel or merchant to advise with—and my reputation as a ship master depending upon the measures I persued &c."

Captain Cobb had landed in France in the middle of the French Revolution. "All was arnachy & confusion, the galliotine in continual operation, their streets & publick squars drenched with human blood. I noted down 1,000 persons that I saw beheaded by that *infernal* machine, and probably saw as many more that I did not note down—men, women, preists & laymen of all ages and finally, before I left the country, I saw Robertspeirs head taken off by the same Machine—"

Quite the experience for this Cape Cod–born boy.

Cobb had to think fast about how to save the vessel's cargo. "His concern was indemnification, which France was more than willing to pay in theory, because Americans were thought to be allies" of the French, noted Hill. A man Cobb couldn't locate had confiscated every scrap of important paper that Cobb had aboard, including official documents. Without those papers, "I could not prove any demand for redress upon the government for their violation of our neutrality. It was true my vessel was there, but her cargo of Flour & Rice had been taken out & was daily made into bread, soups, &c &c, for the half starved populace. Without papers I could not even substantiate my claim to an empty ship," Cobb recounted. In the meantime, he and his crew were sent to a "Hotell."

Captain Elijah Cobb of Brewster lived life fully and traveled the world but always returned to his hometown. *Courtesy of North Road Publishing.*

Cobb heard nothing for six weeks, and his anxiety crept northward with each passing day. The American chargé d'affaires in Paris, to whom Cobb had written, expressed sympathy and asked Cobb to be patient, and he was sure all would be sorted out in time. The Tribunal of Commerce, meanwhile, notified Cobb that he had been tried without him knowing he was on trial, "but in that way all business was managed in France at that time."

Unbelievably, the news a translator had delivered to the captain was not bad. "They declared my vessel & cargo to be newtrial [neutral] property…& that, as the cargo was at my disposition, I should be paid for it by the government at prices that might be fixed upon myself & the agent of the government, and an adequate endemnification for my capture, detention, expenditures &c &c." Soon after, a French marine agent met with Cobb, and they agreed on what the cargo was worth: flour at $16.50 and rice at $5.50

(we presume per barrel, per Hill). How the cargo was measured, however, is lost to time. To recoup the value of the cargo, Cobb was given French "bills of exchange," or promissory notes, which after a month, failed to arrive at Cobb's hotel. Frustrated, Cobb sent his vessel home under the command of his first mate, with ballast to steady its sails. Cobb sent along a letter to the owners explaining his dilemma.

Cobb decided to travel to Paris to make his claim, but travel was dangerous. "All horses had been taken into requisition by the government, except those that conveyd national dispatches. There was no other mode of travelling, and it was conterary to law for the mail couriers to take passengers, but my mind was fixed upon going as the only chance of ever accomplishing my business with the French government." Cobb's plan appeared foolproof. He approached the minister of marine for an official copy of "my demands on the government" and had them recorded. Cobb said this precaution was necessary because "losing" papers was a stall tactic the government used to procrastinate in settling its financial affairs. With copies of his papers in hand, and a hired interpreter by his side, Cobb met with Jean Con St. Andre, "a man holding high offices under the Government & reported to be favourably disposed to Americans." St. Andre promised to take care of Cobb's dilemma the next day. Within forty-eight hours, Cobb was en route to Paris in a mail coach, and he carried a pair of pistols for personal protection. "Our carriage was musquet-shot proof, except in front," Cobb noted. The captain did not sleep at all during the journey of 684 miles, despite "a guard of from 12 to 24 mounted horsemen each night, from sunset to sunrise, preceeding & following."

Having guards accompany the mail couriers proved indispensible. On their way to Paris, Captain Cobb and the mail courier discovered the "remains of a Coreir laying in the road, the master, the Postilion & 5 horses dead, laying & mangled & the mail mutilated & scatered in all directions. We were informed, afterwards, that the Coureir was without a guard the evening previous."

Finally, and still in one piece, Captain Cobb's coach arrived in Paris: "It was at 4 o'clock of a beautyfull June morning when the Carriage stopped before the gate of Hotel de Boston & the bell was rung." Cobb had been on the road for nearly seventy-four hours, "during which time I had not lost myself in sleep, taken anything warm upon my stomock, nor used water upon either hands or face."

More trouble lay ahead. French maritime officials in Paris "lost" the copy of Cobb's papers that he had meticulously copied in Brest where the *Jane* had been captured. "It was concluded that they must have been left upon the counter, brushed off, & burned, along with other loose papers."

Advice from an English-speaking French general suggested that Captain Cobb directly appeal to Maximilien François Marie Isidore de Robespierre (1758–1794,) a French lawyer and politician and a leading figure in the French Revolution. Captain Cobb wrote the following note, which was delivered by a servant to Robespierre: "An American citizen, captured by a French frigate on the high seas, requests a personal interview, to lay his grievance before citizen Roberspeire. Very Respectfully, E. Cobb."

Within the hour, Robespierre sent a note back agreeing to "an interview tomorrow at 10 A.M." During their meeting, Robespierre instructed Cobb to return to the same office, "and if he does not produce your papers & finish your business *immediately* he will hear from me again in a way not so pleasing to him." Within a day, Cobb had his papers back, but he had to wait until his bills or promissory note was paid, and that would take at least sixty days. As for Robespierre: a guillotine lopped off his head shortly after his meeting with Cobb. After arriving back in Brest, France, Cobb boarded a vessel for Hamburg, Germany, where a French agent would convert the bills into cash—forty thousand crowns in silver, to be precise.

Cobb's next task was to safeguard the heavy amount of metal cash in his possession. He also boarded the next boat from Hamburg bound for Boston. Cobb "took passage for Boston in the ship *Warren,* Capt. Hodgkins, where we safely arrived after a passage of 54 days. My arrival gave great relief to my owners for, from the accounts they had in France, they doubted the validity of my Bills on Hamburg, & expected I wou'd have to return to France." Far from disgrace, Cobb's adventures "greatly added to my fame as a ship master."

I asked the most recent editor of Cobb's diary, Deborah Hill, what she thought about the good captain, who was the sixth great-grandfather of her husband. "A friend of mine, who read my edition of Elijah's diary (which is easier going than the first, by the way), remarked that he must have been brilliant. And maybe he was, but don't forget, he 'came in through the hause hole,' meaning he learned his trade from the bottom up," Hill clarified. "I'd judge, starting from his first expedition to Surinam as cook and cabin boy to his capture by the French, he'd been training for better than ten years, and learning the economics of trade was as important as learning how to sail a brig."

And oh so clearly, Cobbs's penchant for writing his diary clearly inspired at least one of his grandchildren, Caroline Atherton Dugan, to do the same.

Caroline Atherton Dugan

Of all the literary elegance so apparent in Caroline "Caro" Atherton Dugan's diaries that spanned 1883 to 1878, it is her artful descriptions of nature on Cape Cod that linger in the realm between poetry and art and reveal an enviable nineteenth-century landscape.

From Tuesday, May 19, 1874, when Caro was twenty-one: "Found today green sprigs of money wort striped grass, coral spires of the sorrel, pretty green currant blossoms, milkweed, the pink & white peach & cherry, & silver abele twigs, the small, velvety leaves just uncurling to silvery gray." It's as if her diary-keeping was truly the work of an amateur naturalist. Simply, Caro noticed everything on her nearly daily walks in Brewster. On Sunday, May 31, Caro penned the following: "Oh, the lovely, lovely May! Apple & cherry boughs wreathed & garlanded with snowy bloom, and the horse chestnuts light lanes and avenues with their lantern-like flower clusters. These trees are like great beehives in shape, and standing beneath them we hear the deep continuous hum of bees overhead among the flowers. Dandelions are now tall & rank in aunt Nettie's orchard, but I like better the first golden darlings nestling in the grass. They already are going to seed."

Caroline was the daughter of James and Helen Cobb Dugan, and she was born in Brewster on March 26, 1853. Her mother, Helen, was the daughter of Elijah Cobb, the brilliant sea captain. She was formally educated and was qualified to teach kindergarten, but her career instead was spent as a governess to five children in Brookline, Massachusetts, for over twenty-five years. But each summer, after she temporarily left the household of

Henry and Margaret Whitney, she returned to the Brewster homestead, where she immersed herself in community affairs and perfected her skills as an amateur photographer under a gentleman, Cornelius Chenery, who boarded in the family home.

Dugan was a founding member of the Brewster Ladies' Library and served as its first librarian. Her passion for words and appreciation of nature were predominant themes in her diary since Caroline came of age during the Victorian era, when British adoration of the natural world spilled over to American circles. Indeed, in 1874, Caro, who was an avid reader, was undoubtedly influenced by three of the books she listed as having read that year, all of which were nature-driven: *Walden* and *A Week on the Concord & Merrimac Rivers* by Henry David Thoreau and W.E. Channing's *Thoreau: The Poet-Naturalist.* Is it too much to assume that Thoreau himself was her muse?

Like it did Thoreau, simply being outdoors filled Caro with obvious joy. On Sunday, May 24, 1874, it was the grass that enchanted her. "One could lie on its green couch for hours, gazing up through the silvery mist of abele foliage, watching the yellow-birds flash in & out of blossoming fruit trees, the homely spotted toad hop out from the grass to gaze at you with bright intent eyes, the lovely spring toilets of pansy & periwinkle, violet & dandelion; and hearing the rustle of leaves, the winds in the pine trees, the hum of bees, cawing of crows, laughter of the bobolink and all the varied notes of robin, bluebird, cat-bird, pee wee, oriole, quail, sparrow, & swallow."

On Saturday, June 13, Caro was "out early for flowers. The grass heavily silvered with dew, each grass blade strung with diamonds, rubies, emeralds, topaz, and I was soon as richly adorned with jewels as a princess, while low wet boughs of trees shook delicious little showers on my hair and face. I filled my hands with cypress vine, wild geranium, and spider wort deep purple and violet and white. The fields are white with daisies and golden with buttercups, and there are often great stretches of sweet blossoming clover."

And so progressed the summer of 1875 on Cape Cod for Caroline A. Dugan, and on Thursday, August 31, Caro spent the afternoon with Relief Paine of Brewster, who at sixteen had fallen down the stairs, resulting in paralysis and blindness. "She had ready for me a quantity of marsh rosemary, blue and fresh." As always, Caro's love of nature shows through as the summer winds wane and lean into fall. "The first of August, slender spires of golden rod appear and the first white asters; at its close they are in full glory. Pink spirea, purple milkweed, butter & eggs, heavy golden tansy, cardinal flowers, pink hibiscus, feathery reed grass & darker foxtail grasses are August children. In the garden grow thyme, nasturtiums, sweet peas, double scarlet geranium, garden asters of purple, red & white, sweet alyssum, mignonette, and four o'clocks."

It's clear the change of seasons enthralled Caro as she drove through the woods between two ponds on Friday, October 16. "The road lays across a narrow strip of land, bright with the autumnal beauty of trees & shrubs & alder berries, which separated the two ponds. On the right, the water rippled brightly on a narrow, sandy beach, & stretched wide & far away to a line of low sand cliffs misty in the distance. On the left was a smaller, shallower piece of water, red with the reflection of woods that crowded close to its margin, and near the shore spread with a network of lily leaves, silver in the sunshine, through which tall rushes pushed their way and red water grasses waved."

Caro's diary is more than the chronicle of days by an articulate, educated woman. I think it's important to note that Caro's descriptions of the rural and natural Cape Cod landscape afford contemporary ecologists an accurate botanical inventory of native plants, which is important in conservation circles that value indigenous flowers, plants and grasses.

It was evident that Caro treasured nature and people. On June 2, 1874, Caro "walked to Relief's. The poor girl has had another of her bad attacks (the last was four years ago) and could not speak or move hand & head. I chattered away to her, telling everything that I thought might interest her." On Monday, June 15, Caro strolled back to Relief's house. "She is better & can talk to me again. Most beautiful to see & remember are the sweet purity of her face and her lovely, patient smile." Caro notes in many diary entries that she spends a lot of mornings with Relief, just talking.

On Friday, September 29, 1876, Relief turned thirty. "Half her life has been spent in that little darkened room," recounted Caro. For the next two days, Caro would visit Relief once again.

Caroline Dugan composed two large diaries, according to Kay Dorn, who edited the volumes on behalf of the Brewster Ladies' Library. The first volume included 1873 through 1876, and she began writing them at the age of twenty. Her thoughts and general rhythm of life are reflected in the second volume, composed in 1877 and 1878. It wasn't until 1941, Dorn says, specifically on October 1, that Caroline's diaries were accessioned at a meeting of the Brewster Ladies' Library Association. At that meeting, an association officer was instructed to "write to Mrs. Frank B. Duveneck thanking her for the gifts of Miss Dugan's books and letters." Mrs. Duveneck had called Caro her governess for many years, and following Dugan's death on March 26, 1941, her "official papers" had finally come home.

The Gravest of Tales

Their bones are six feet under in any one of over one hundred cemeteries on Cape Cod, from Bourne to Provincetown. What was left of their dreams, worries, achievements and disappointments were laid to rest on flat, sculpted terrain and in silent tombs tucked into small hillsides in Falmouth's Oak Grove Cemetery, the West Baptist Cemetery, the Old Burying Ground in Orleans or dozens of other sacred places. "I would put the number of gravestones in the 15 towns on Cape Cod through 1900 at about 40,000," detailed Robert Paine Carlson, chair of the Eastham Cemetery Commission and a leading authority on gravestones. "There are probably another ten thousand burials without gravestones," he added. "Some unmarked burials never had gravestones, and some had gravestones, which had disappeared."

But is there a hidden value to cemeteries in our contemporary culture beyond serving as the physical resting place of their full-time residents?

"For me, it's a peaceful place to be," noted historian Nancy Viall Shoemaker of West Barnstable, a longtime authority on Cape Cod cemeteries. She calls them "a place of art. Obviously a place of history and genealogy, but also a place of art, nature and even wildlife," she added.

Shoemaker's words were reassuring, because I've always felt walking through a cemetery was intrusive or disrespectful to the dead. Now I realize the quietude there is restorative and contemplative. Shoemaker insists cemeteries allow us to "discover the culture of different times." She adds, "It's not just the two dates on the stone, it's everything in between. I love

Above: In Yarmouth's Woodside Cemetery, most graves date to the early nineteenth or late eighteenth centuries. *Courtesy of Theresa M. Barbo.*

Left: This grave at Woodside Cemetery belongs to little Norrie, a child whose family lived at the nearby SandySide estate. *Courtesy of Theresa M. Barbo.*

when there is a hint of what had transpired between those [birth and death] dates, such as a listing of their occupation or how they died."

Robert Paine Carlson's website, capecodgravestones.com, is a virtual online university that I urge you to visit. The mission of the site is "to photograph and display the most interesting old gravestones in Barnstable County before they are lost to the ravages of time. A related goal is to provide reasonably complete gravestone records from the earliest in 1683 up to 1900 for all Barnstable County cemeteries. The website is complete to 1880 for most cemeteries and many cemeteries are complete to 1900."

When Benjamin Fessenden of Sandwich died in 1746, he was buried in Sandwich at the Burying Ground Cemetery with a unique tabletop-style tombstone:

> *Here mouldering lies the*
> *Reverend Benjamin Fessenden*
> *who was born at Cambridge June 3ᵈ*
> *1701 graduated at Harvard College*
> *ordained minister at Sandwich*
> *June 12ᵗʰ 1722 and deceased*
> *Aug 7ᵗʰ 1746 Age 45. Concerning whom it may*
> *with truth be said that he was an instance of early piety,*
> *and in his youth made swift advances in valuable knowledge;*
> *that, having used his best endeavors*
> *to prepare himself for the service of the Sanctuary,*
> *he was introduced into it with general approbation,*
> *and employed in it to the good of others and his own comfort;*
> *that not only as a divine he was useful,*
> *but as a discreet and successful physician,*
> *and that, after a long exercise of fortitude, readiness*
> *and patience under weakness and various bodily infirmities,*
> *he gave up the ghost with tranquility,*
> *and rests from his trouble and labours.*

When Temperance Nye of Falmouth died in 1794, her bereaved parents commissioned the following tombstone:

> *Memento mortis*
> *In Memory of*
> *Miss Temperance Nye dau*

of Cap Ebenezer Nye, &
Mrs Fear his wife who
died May 31ˢᵗ 1794 In
her 21ˢᵗ Year

The virgin graces bloom'd upon her cheek Her mind was virtuous and her temper meek Confin'd in dust, her tender body lies Till called to meet her pious soul

No two gravestones are alike. Chiseled by artisans from granite, marble and even slate, these ancient tombstones are in clear danger of disintegration by weather and fungus, which render text illegible. Slate is, for example, naturally compressed stone, and when snow melts in between the layers or rain pours down them, it slowly but steadily separates the layers. Periods of extreme cold followed by the thawing process can erode the layers, too. Weed whackers and lawn mowers bump into stone monuments, Shoemaker adds, and help in the disintegration process. "Good-quality slate stones do not erode, but they tend to split or break. Marble stones that became popular in the nineteenth century are eroded by acid rain. Sandstone or brownstone gravestones do not stand up well to weathering," explained Carlson. "Granite, which is much more durable, was not used until the late 1800s. Vandalism also takes its toll. Well-cared-for cemeteries seem to have less vandalism," he clarified.

But while they exist, and while you are able to read them, do so. Think of gravestones as an open-air art exhibit. Depending on when they were carved, earlier headstones have skulls and crossbones. Later generations of carvers used cherubs with wings on their design, and in an even later period, willow trees bent over with an urn design complement the artwork.

Famous carvers include Nathaniel Holmes of Barnstable, the county's first resident carver who is credited with crafting well over 1,300 tombstones in the early nineteenth century.

In his role as chair of the Eastham Cemetery Commission, Carlson spends "considerable time" giving tours and talking with visitors on genealogical expeditions for ancestors. "There is much discussion of what was it like back then. Were there Indians? Were there doctors? Why did the wives have so many children? What were the houses like? How many people lived in the area? Were they farmers or fishermen or what?" Carlson has experienced seeing different groups of visitors connect over the grave of a shared ancestor, "especially graves of *Mayflower* passengers."

The Learning Curve

O n September 9, 1897, in the middle of Hyannis, William A. Baldwin, an Ivy League–trained educator, proudly watched as thirty-two students walked into the Hyannis State Normal School to begin their first term there.

The Hyannis campus was the eighth normal school in the commonwealth, enacted into law in 1838 to ensure that well-versed teachers led public schools. The model was based on a French system, *écoles normale*, which put much value on teaching as a necessary and respected profession. A year later, in July 1839, the first such teachers' college opened in Lexington. Less than a year later, in June 1894, according to Bridgewater State University, a sum of $75,000 was appropriated for a normal school in Barnstable County, with Hyannis coming out on top of other towns that requested the honor of hosting.

Principal Baldwin oversaw a small faculty of three other fellow professors. Bertha M. Brown taught future teachers biology, mathematics and English. Classes in chemistry, mineralogy and drawing were led by Sara T. Oliver, and Edmund F. Sawyer oversaw instruction in "vocal music." Baldwin was not merely an administrator. He taught history of education, pedagogy and psychology. The original campus consisted of four buildings, including the normal school, dorms, the principal's residence and the training school building. "The normal school building contained recitation rooms, lecture rooms, laboratories and a gymnasium. The dormitory building contained twenty-six rooms for students, two for teachers, one for a matron, three for servants, a guest chamber, a

A class picture of students attending the Hyannis State Normal School. *Courtesy of the W.B. Nickerson Archives, Cape Cod Community College.*

The ladies' basketball team at the Hyannis State Normal School. *Courtesy of the W.B. Nickerson Archives, Cape Cod Community College.*

parlor, a dining room, a kitchen, a laundry, a pantry, a servant's sitting room, and a storeroom," according to data compiled by Bridgewater State University (BSU) for an exhibit on normal schools.

The normal school went coed until the early 1920s. After that, only women were admitted, but young male teachers began attending again after 1933.

We often think of early twentieth-century education in terms of the proverbial one-room schoolhouse. But these were enlightened times. Future teachers trained at the Hyannis campus for two years until 1899, when a third and fourth year of study were offered. By September 1930, a three-year diploma offering "broader fields" of study was offered. And in 1931, a bachelor of science in education for future elementary school teachers was conferred on graduates following a four-year course of study. By September 1933, training for advanced educators who prepared to teach on the high school, or secondary, level had been introduced. "Barnstable Junior and Senior High Schools were collaborators, allowing student teachers access for observation and practice teaching," cited BSU.

In 1937, the Massachusetts commissioner of education granted the Hyannis Normal School the right to offer summer sessions leading to a master's degree, the first of which was conferred in 1939.

But the Hyannis Normal School wasn't all work. Long before Title IX and other legally mandated restrictions to enable women to play sports, the Hyannis Normal School offered team sports, including basketball, to female students. This formal study of physical training began in 1899 under a teacher named Eva A. Hickox. Annie S. Crowell, who graduated from Hyannis Normal and stayed on its faculty for the next four decades, succeeded her.

Then came the downside years. Lack of funding and diminishing numbers of students threatened the Hyannis State Normal School. The nail in the coffin was World War II, when enrollment plummeted. The Massachusetts Maritime Academy (MMA) was granted permission in 1942 to share the campus, and by 1944 MMA has assumed complete control. Following a recommendation by the commissioner of education that the Hyannis State Normal School be temporarily closed following the summer session of 1944, steps were taken to permanently close the school once Massachusetts governor Leverett Saltonstall agreed to those terms.

Cutting-edge subjects such as navigation were part of the curricula at Pine Grove Seminary in Harwich. *Courtesy of the W.B. Nickerson Archives, Cape Cod Community College.*

If the Hyannis State Normal School (1897–1944) was *the* training institution for future educators, an earlier school that had opened in Harwich in 1844 for high school students proved that cutting-edge education was not limited to the twentieth or even the twenty-first centuries.

Sidney Brooks (1813–1887), a Harwich-born graduate of Amherst College, was teaching school in Chatham, where he recognized that for public school students in his hometown of Harwich, formal educational opportunities ended at eighth grade. He purchased for an "Academy or High School in the central part of (Harwich)…to erect a building for that purpose," according to the Harwich Historical Society. The elegant Greek Revival structure that still stands today opened its doors in 1844; it was also known as Pine Grove Seminary or Brooks Academy.

Costing upward of four dollars a term, Brooks Academy was coed, and among the unique offerings in coursework were navigation and surveying, English, French, Latin, Greek, piano and drawing. One hidden element to the Brooks Academy story on Cape Cod was its ability to successfully segregate its classrooms. "By the turn of the 20th century, America had become a melting pot," according to the Harwich Historical Society. "Harwich was no exception. French, Irish, Cape Verdeans, and Finns joined the English and

By the early 1900s, demographics on Cape Cod represented many ethnicities. *Courtesy of the W.B. Nickerson Archives, Cape Cod Community College.*

Scots who already inhabited the village. By this time the Native American population had all but disappeared."

In 1869, the Town of Harwich bought the building from Sidney Brooks. In 1880, Harwich High School opened its doors there, with additions to the south side in 1909 and on the west side of the building in 1929. By 1988, after a few more incarnations, the building housed Brooks Academy Museum and is home to the Harwich Historical Society.

There's No Place Like Home

I t's one thing to visit one's hometown after a long absence. It's another to celebrate one's hometown, and there's a difference between the two.

One hidden gemstone is that the very first town in Massachusetts to *formally* seek to honor its civic ties and tradition was Harwich, which supported a state law passed in 1902 to set "aside one week each year for the

Few towns on Cape Cod threw a parade quite like Harwich. *Courtesy of the W.B. Nickerson Archives, Cape Cod Community College.*

observance," according to the Harwich Historical Society (HHS). Fanfare included a parade on Main Street, competitive games and sports, music and, according to HHS, a monstrous clambake.

The *Harwich Independent* newspaper wrote in its July 2, 1902 edition: "Old Home Week means much to Harwich and if each person will show an interest and put forth a little effort, this will be the biggest week Harwich ever knew. Arthur F. Cahoon is offering inducements to encourage the display of flags and bunting. Any one who wants a flag can get *it* of him at wholesale price which is 35 percent from regular retail price. Leave your orders as early as possible."

Clearly Harwich was a trendsetter. On June 21, 1904, the *Harwich Independent* noted, "Other towns of the right arm of Massachusetts have also adopted Old Home Week ideas since reorganizing the importance and true meaning of such an observance."

A Nor'easter's Familiar Rage, Sea Talk and a Famous Reunion

The 1952 rescue of thirty-two sailors off a sinking oil tanker by a four-man Coast Guard crew aboard the motor lifeboat *CG36500* is the stuff of local legend. Hands down, if anyone on Cape Cod mentions the "Coast Guard" and "storm" in one sentence, they are probably talking about the *Pendleton* rescue. The *Pendleton* was a 503-foot tanker, and its sister ship was the *Fort Mercer*. Both vessels snapped in two during a nor'easter on February 17, 1952. A day later, that four-man Coast Guard crew aboard the *36500*—which included Coxswain Bernie Webber, Engineman Andy Fitzgerald, Ervin Maske and Richard Livesey—accomplished what I could only call a miracle. Their trip through hellish high seas went against every shred of logic in maritime circles, and the odds were stacked too high against them to survive. But they did.

What you're about to read is a series of essays in which new or updated data is revealed about this iconic mission.

Cape Cod, Massachusetts, January 27, 2015; 12:42 a.m.

On this morning as I write, the soul of a ferocious winter has unleashed a tempest. Nor'easter winds have unfurled bands of snow over swirling waves and frozen shores. There is no let-up in the winds, only the sound of one long rumble from the heavens above.

The legendary *CG36500* sits at a dock at Rock Harbor in Orleans. *Courtesy of Theresa M. Barbo.*

This is what it was like on February 18, 1952, when a nor'easter snapped two 503-foot oil tankers, the *Pendleton* and *Fort Mercer,* in two off Chatham, resulting in the rescue of seventy of eighty-four seamen from those vessels. The rescue of thirty-two mariners from the *Pendleton* by a four-man crew from the *CG36500,* a 36-foot motor rescue lifeboat, is today recognized as the greatest small boat rescue in Coast Guard history.

Coincidentally, I'm writing about that very storm that occurred nearly sixty-three years ago, as a similar gale hollers its presence outside. And what lies hidden in plain sight is not merely the sheer miracle of the rescue itself but also the unique relationship between men and one very special boat.

For two men who grew up in Chatham and were mere boys in 1952 on the night of the *Pendleton* Disaster, even today the fury of a nor'easter stirs up uneasy remembrances of the '52 nor'easter. I had asked William "Bill" Cummings, a former naval officer, pilot and now a business owner in Indianapolis, for his remembrances of that night.

In an e-mail on January 26 at 8:20 a.m., Cummings remarked:

> *It is ironic that I will be writing about the wreck of the* Pendleton *during a very similar storm that is hitting New England and Cape Cod tonight*

and tomorrow. The weather forecast for Hyannis for 1 AM tomorrow morning is very similar to the conditions that caused the wreck of the Pendleton: *Northeast gale force winds, very low ceilings, heavy blowing snow, and restricted visibility. If you can capture the feelings of the storm tonight and tomorrow morning, that would be very similar to the conditions on the afternoon and evening of February 18, 1952.*

Spoken like a naval officer, yes?

Earlier this evening, another e-mail arrived, this one from Richard "Dick" Ryder of Eastham, LCDR, USN (Ret.), who included me on a small message chain with more thoughts about the nor'easter of '52 and brilliant comparisons to 2015. "This storm appears to be much more powerful than the one back in 1952 that trashed the *Pendleton* and the *Fort Mercer*," explained Ryder. "According to NOAA tonight, forecast sea heights are in the twenty- to thirty-foot range for this event. Maybe higher offshore, where the larger CG cutters were back then, offering assistance to the *Fort Mercer*. Nowhere near the seventy-foot seas that some folks think the *CG36500* encountered en route to the stern of the SS *Pendleton*, which was maybe a mile offshore."

Dick Ryder was only a kid in 1952, but he remembers that night well. "As a young boy of twelve, I was fascinated with the chatter back and forth between the Chatham CG Station, Nan Mike Fox 29 (not Station Chatham as they call it now) and the Motor Lifeboat, NFDS—Nan Fox Dog Sugar. There were gaps in the conversation, as apparently Bernie had shut off the radio to avoid having to deal with the senior officers on the cutters offshore," remembered Ryder. "If you look closely at the photos of the boat returning back then, you can see part of the NFDS painted on the forward compartment. There was no *CG36500* lettering anywhere on the boat," he added. Today, Ryder is coxswain of the *CG36500*, and the principal responsibilities of its care and maintenance fall to him, as well as to Donnie St. Pierre of Chatham. For decades, both St. Pierre and Ryder have devoted countless hours to this vessel.

As the storm battled Cape Cod outside, Bill Cummings wrote the following remembrance of 1952 from his home in Indianapolis. His recollection as a child of the 1952 Coast Guard rescue adds to the small album of existing eyewitness accounts of Chatham residents. The night of the rescue, young Cummings was in sixth grade at the Chatham Junior High School, just three months shy of his twelfth birthday.

The family's home, Spindrift, on Old Wharf Road in North Chatham, which still stands today, had a great view of the water, with no houses

As a twelve-year-old, William Cummings saw the mortally wounded *Pendleton* drift by his Chatham home. *Courtesy of William Cummings.*

on its east side, offering an unimpeded view. Cummings describes the unique terrain that "descends downhill to the east to about ten feet above mean sea level, then takes a 90° turn to the north and climbs to the top of another hill which is probably sixty to seventy feet above sea level. There were also no houses on the land east of the saltmarsh that would have obstructed our vantage point. We had a perfect view across Pleasant Bay, the Outer Beach/North Beach, and the ocean beyond. The ocean surf was approximately three-quarters of a mile from where we stood."

At about 4:30 p.m., Cummings, his mother and two others drove to the crest of Old Wharf Road to see if they could see the vessel that was blaring its horn, which turned out to be the *Pendleton*. They were about two miles north of Chatham Light. He said daylight was "fading fast…But as the weather was rainy, with low clouds and a lot of wind, sunset was somewhat meaningless." Cummings certainly didn't know a second ship was involved, nor did anyone know the name of the vessel that turned out to be the *Pendleton*.

With a boy's memories and the expertise of the retired naval officer that he is, Cummings now estimated that the winds that night off Chatham were between fifty and seventy knots, about fifty-seven to eighty miles per hour. The rain pelted their faces. "Visibility was possibly three miles with rain and wind blowing hard enough to lift the surface water from Pleasant Bay, as it often does during hurricanes," he explained.

Our vantage point was approximately three-quarters of a mile back from the ocean side of the outer beach, and probably two to three miles from the target of our curiosity. Much to our surprise, after straining to see through the winter gale, we could make out what later was determined to be the stern section of the SS Pendleton. *The image of the ship was unclear through the mist and rain, but it clearly was the remains of a large ship in serious distress approximately two miles offshore. The stern section of the ship was facing northeast…the stern was sunken deep into the water, and the angle of the deck was probably ten to twenty degrees from the stern, facing toward where the bow had been.*

Cumming said the *Pendleton*'s hull rose and sank with the seas as it slowly drifted south along the beach toward Chatham Light and Chatham's inlet. The *Pendleton*'s foghorn rhythmically cried for help through the corridors of gale winds and fell unattended at the doorstep of North Beach. Cummings said his group did not see "any lights or souls on board the ship" from where they stood.

"The tide was coming in (flood tide), which means that the current was flowing from north to south along North Beach, from Provincetown toward Chatham, and toward Monomoy Point. Pushed by the current, massive wind and waves, the ship was drifting southward at probably two or three knots per hour along the beach," he recalled. Until the drifting *Pendleton* left their sight, Cummings's group watched the ship for about twenty minutes.

"As a young boy, I was calculating that the *Pendleton* was drawing probably forty to fifty feet of water because the hull was substantially submerged at the stern and the ship would surely run aground soon. I guessed the normal draft at about twenty-eight feet. I also felt any rescue attempts would be futile because of the size of the surf, the high winds and the low visibility," he explained over six decades later. "As a young boy, I had read about Breeches buoys being fired from the beach for rescue attempts. However, at that time, the hull was drawing too much water to be close enough to shore for a successful 'off-the-beach' rescue. I did not believe any rescue attempt would be possible and the Coast Guard would just have to wait until the storm subsided. The ship would probably run aground off Monomoy Point, or capsize and entire crew would be lost. I am not certain what time the courageous crew of the Chatham Coast Guard thirty-six-foot motor whaleboat departed from the Chatham Fish Pier (Aunt Lydia's Cove), or even if they left from Chatham Fish Pier, as opposed to Stage Harbor," said the retired naval officer. "In any event, the trip to the

Pendleton rescue point had to be hell on earth. The trip from Stage Harbor would have been five miles west, twelve miles south and then twelve miles northeast into the raging thirty-foot seas. The trip from Aunt Lydia's Cove would have been about eight miles south, and then three to four miles eastward through gigantic surf which would destroy virtually any conventional boat," Cummings recounted.

"As far as the timing goes, our observation of the *Pendleton* around 4:30 p.m. to 5:00 p.m. coincides with the actual rescue that apparently took place two or three miles east of the old Chatham inlet around 7:00 or 8:00 p.m. The rescue point would have occurred about six or seven miles farther southward down the coast from our observation point. Historically, the hull of the *Pendleton* finally came to rest about six or seven miles south of the rescue point, about two miles offshore (east) of Monomoy Point, in water about thirty-five feet deep. The hull rested there for many years, and was a navigational fix for decades. The ship leaked minor amounts of fuel oil into the ocean for years and years," he said.

"One of my greatest regrets is that I was not taken to Chatham Fish Pier to observe the return of the gallant motor whaleboat crew and the rescued sailors," Cummings remembered. But he wasn't alone. So many people, especially men who were boys in 1952, regret not being at the dock that night.

"Unfortunately, a lack of information about current events, on a timely basis, was scarce in the '50s. If only my father had been home! I am certain we guys would have gone to the Fish Pier. No doubt, Mother felt standing in the rain with a young daughter and son for an unknown period of time, waiting for the lifeboat to return to shore, was not an option," he said.

Cummings insists:

> *The rescue itself was spectacular! To be able to approach a pitching and rolling steel hull, fifty-foot waves, gale force winds, with a very small, poorly maneuverable lifeboat, while attempting to rescue people who were clinging to and climbing down a rope ladder, is almost impossible. I performed such maneuvers while in the Navy, with similar motor whaleboats, but all in reasonably calm seas. These maneuvers are still exceedingly challenging and very dangerous. An even more spectacular aspect about the* Pendleton *rescue was the coxswain's ability to locate the sea buoy that marks the entrance to Chatham inlet without sophisticated navigational tools such as GPS or LORAN receivers. I believe it was God's divine intervention*

that allowed the skipper of the motor whaleboat to find his way back to Chatham inlet.

I've experienced hundreds of hours fishing in Chatham inlet, around the sandbars and surf, and find the inlet an exceedingly dangerous place. Over the years, dozens of fishermen have perished in Chatham inlet. The question remains as to how an overloaded rescue motor whaleboat, with so much weight in the bow, with gigantic surf breaking all around, could navigate Chatham inlet at night. As for my belief about why the Pendleton and the Fort Mercer ships broke in half, the rumors at the time were as follows:

Before World War II, ships were built as single units in gigantic shipyards that could accommodate ship hulls lengths of up to one thousand feet. During that war, in order to build ships in huge numbers, the industry incorporated many modern industrial techniques from the era of mass production. Apparently the Liberty ships were built in smaller shipyards that could not accommodate large ships. Therefore, they were built in two sections: the bow and the stern. Then the bow and stern were mated together upon completion of the separate units. The ships were welded together, rather than the traditional riveting technique. The life expectancy of Liberty ships during the war was measured in terms of months, rather than years.

Many of the Liberty ships were sold to private industry at the end of World War II for very little money. They were war surplus and perhaps in 1952 even beyond their life expectancy. The ships were manufactured to be expendable, because their life expectancy in the North Atlantic against the German submarines was perceived to be very short. They were not built for longevity or strength, as demonstrated by the fact that two Liberty ships failed on the same night under the same conditions at approximately the same location. My recent research confirms the rumors that we had heard in the 1950s. The British who needed a massive number of steamships to support its war effort originally created the concept of Liberty ships. The British originally contracted with U.S. shipyards to build 60 ships for the British and the United States ordered 200 ships. Ultimately, 2,751 Liberty ships were built in the United States in seventeen different shipyards.

Henry J. Kaiser pioneered the new ship building techniques. Kaiser developed methods for fabricating and mass-producing Liberty ships. Components were built all across the U.S. and transported to shipyards where they could be assembled in record time. As a publicity stunt, a Liberty ship was built in four days, fifteen hours and twenty-nine minutes. Near the end of the Second World War, the seventeen shipyards were turning out one new ship every day. To regress and also document the power of the sea, the following is a personal account of a near disaster, while I was in the Navy.

In November 1964, I was the deck officer on the USS Blandy (DD 943), a Forest Sherman class destroyer built in the mid-1950s. We were returning to Newport, Rhode Island, from the Mediterranean. Due to a misguided set of orders to avoid a late fall hurricane traveling up the east coast of the United States, our orders were to sail south by the Azores, then due west towards the Caribbean, and then due north up the middle of the Atlantic ocean towards Nova Scotia. The barometric pressure dropped to 28.56 inches of mercury, which is a very low reading, indicating a very severe low-pressure area. Ironically our ship was caught in the equivalent of "The Perfect Storm."

Our convoy consisted of the USS Essex, a Second World War aircraft carrier that had been converted to submarine warfare, and seven destroyers. When we finally turned southwest back towards the continental United States, we faced gale force winds, blinding snow, and 100-foot waves, waves so big the surf at the top rolled over the entire ship with an estimated depth of water on deck to be 10 or 15 feet. Our 442-foot ship would climb a monstrous wave like we were surfboarding off Waikiki Beach. At the wave top, the breaking wave would engulf the entire ship as the ship groaned with wrenching pain of an unsupported bow, while it crashed again into the next monstrous sea.

As the result of the twisting and pounding, our ship sustained numerous broken ribs about one hundred feet back from the bow, and spent a year in the Boston naval shipyard being rebuilt. We also lost a twenty-six-foot motor whaleboat, the commodore's thirty-four-foot motorboat and virtually all of our twenty-four inflatable life rafts. The aircraft carrier USS Essex sustained such incredible damage from the storm; the ship was decommissioned and mothballed. These war ships were manufactured to sustain far more stress and damage than the Liberty ships.

Because of the twisting and crashing which Coast Guard rescue vessels encounter in the surf and at sea, new Coast Guard motor whaleboats are made with RIB construction, which incorporates rubber flotation chambers around a rigid hull, to provide far more buoyancy and less rigidity than more conventional designed hulls. We have learned a great deal about the construction of seagoing vessels over the past one hundred years.

Jack Downey, a retired Coast Guard master chief, delivering a lecture on the *Pendleton* at the Maine Maritime Academy. *Courtesy of Theresa M. Barbo.*

SEA TALK

A vitally untold chapter in the greatest small boat rescue in Coast Guard history comes from retired master chief John E. "Jack" Downey, a good friend who also knew all four crewmen aboard the *CG36500*. Jack has also driven the *36500* and was instrumental in the vessel's upkeep during his tenure as officer-in-charge (OIC) at CG Station Chatham.

On May 8, 2009, Jack delivered a speech at Station Chatham to mark the decommissioning of the service's forty-four-foot fleet and its last lifeboat, the *CG44301*. Jack knew the forty-four well. In July 1968, he qualified as a coxswain. Regarding the vessel's limitations: "It can operate in thirty-foot seas, twenty-foot surf and breaking waves and fifty-knot sustained winds," Downey recalled. (In an earlier era, the Coast Guard used numerical identifications and not actual names for its rescue vessels. Before the forty-fours took to the water in the early 1960s, the Coast Guard used thirty-six-foot motor lifeboats, as in the *36500*.) Keep in mind that Bernie Webber, the coxswain of the *36500* in '52, had taken a brand-new forty-four-foot rescue motor lifeboat on its sea trials and, in fact, helped design and evaluate the vessel. The irony here is that Bernie had just passed on in

January 2009, and his services were held the weekend that the very boat he helped design was formally decommissioned.

At any rate, as Jack was formally recognizing the decommissioning of the last of the forty-four-foot fleet, his speech reminded the largely Coast Guard audience there to "remember your own limitations and that of your crew." His speech centered on "sea talk" and the intangible "relationship" (my words, not his) that a man has with a boat. It got me thinking that the *36500* might be considered a fifth crewman because without it, the mission to save the surviving crew of the *Pendleton* could not have happened. Downey also said:

> *Always remember that the motor lifeboat will only perform as well as the crew that mans it.*
>
> *Always remember that the endurance of a motor lifeboat is far greater than the endurance of the crew.*
>
> *Always remember the vessel will talk to you (sea talk) and will let you know what it likes and dislikes by the way it handles and reacts in a seaway, currents and shallow water to include the effects of the wind. The coxswain must continuously recognize, adjust, correct and anticipate the posture of the vessel, to accommodate its likes and overcome its dislikes through proper use of the throttle and rudder.*
>
> *Always remember that the motor lifeboat will compensate if you make a mistake—it will scare you and save you if you stay with the boat.*
>
> *Remember that the only time we have trouble with boats is when we put people on them.*
>
> *Lastly, always remember that the sea will decide who is qualified and who is not—the motor lifeboat [more] often than not is the referee.*

Jack ended his speech with the further wisdom that the thirty-six-foot motor lifeboats, as in the *CG36500*, "projected improved features and capabilities for the forty-four-foot motor lifeboat, and the forty-four-foot motor lifeboat projected improved features and capabilities for the forty-seven-foot motor lifeboat." The sum of all, Downey clarified, has provided the outstanding footprint for the forty-seven-foot motor lifeboat that's in use today.

We hear so much about that outstanding Coast Guard crew that rescued the *Pendleton* survivors that the mission's fifth crew member, the vessel itself, goes unheralded. "The *CG36500* is a Gold Lifesaving Medal motor lifeboat," Downey reminds us. "This motor lifeboat has displayed and demonstrated its can-do pedigree above and beyond all motor lifeboats of her commissioned class. The *CG36500* has taken on an individual character and soul, bonded to and by, those four heroic Coastguardsmen who manned her in rescuing thirty-two survivors and saving the lives of thirty-six individuals," he said.

A FAMOUS REUNION

Another huge part of the story that's been largely neglected is how people outside select Coast Guard circles came to know about this rescue in the first place. I attribute this to an event held in 2002 that was dreamed up by a Coast Guard captain.

During his tenure as Group Woods Hole commander, Captain W. Russell Webster made it a habit to visit Coast Guard facilities around the district, including the famous Chatham station. There, OIC John E. "Jack" Downey held a pinning ceremony for his successor. The idea was to mix the pins of legendary OIC Bernie Webber with those of a new OIC. This piqued Webster's curiosity, and he began to learn more about the 1952 rescue. "Master Chief Downey had introduced me to Bernie, who had remained relevant with his successor generations of Guardsmen by returning to the Chatham station each summer to listen to today's Coast Guardsmen's stories," remembered Webster. "I committed to learning more about their stories and memorializing their great accomplishments through writing and lectures. Then 9/11 happened, and despite the horrific workload every serviceman experienced shortly thereafter, I knew that hallmarking the *CG36500* crew's historic fiftieth anniversary was the right thing to do. The Coast Guard of 2001 was eager to embrace its heroes past and present," he added.

Webster began to get to work, laying out ideas to a small committee and tapping his network of contacts to help reach the right folks. The three-day reunion would begin with a day in Boston at District 1 Headquarters and end with two days on Cape Cod. Little did he know that the event to be held five months later would generate so much publicity and goodwill and form the starting metric for future books, memorials, a leadership lecture series and even an $81 million vessel.

But before any of those things happened, the reunion itself needed to be planned and executed, and it started with an earnest and sustained attempt to get all four lifesavers together: coxswain Bernie Webber, second engineer Andy Fitzgerald, Richard Livesey and Ervin Maske. Webber had perfectly

Bernie Webber relaxes at dinner in 2002 with Captain W. Russell Webster (center) and Captain James Murray (right). *Courtesy of Theresa M. Barbo.*

good reasons for not wanting to make the trek up from his retirement home in Florida. Back in '52, after the rescue, the Coast Guard had trotted Bernie out in front of audiences in a PR campaign, which made him uncomfortable. Plus, he felt his crew wasn't getting the degree of attention he was, which seemed unfair to them.

It took Captain Webster several attempts before Webber delivered a tentative yes. But Webber had conditions before he would leave Florida to come to Boston. First, all the other guys also had to say yes, and Ervin, Richard and Andy agreed. Second, the Coast Guard had to pay travel expenses not only for the crew members but for their families, too. Captain Webster assured Webber that this would be taken care of, which it was. Webber's main gripe was that in '52, the Gold Medal families were largely excluded from any ceremonies, and he didn't want history to repeat itself.

Webster explained:

> *Truth be told, the type of recognition they received after their famous rescue mortified the heroes of 1952. I think they gave most of the credit for the rescue to God, divine intervention and luck and shunned the drudgery of the Coast Guard's leadership hauling them in front of the media as they were*

in May 1952. So, in part, the four reluctant heroes contributed to the story's somewhat original obscure nature. With time, Bernie published his 1985 Chatham, the Lifeboatman, *which remains the seminal guide for the storytelling on the night of the rescue. Other authors, including Captain Charles Hathaway in* From Highland to Hammerhead *(2000) paid homage to the rescue, but the Coast Guard, for the most part, was content to view their history like its earlier ethos—"You Have to Go Out, But You Don't Have to Come Back." Times and leaders changed at the highest levels, and in 2007, the Coast Guard published its top ten rescues of all time, rightly establishing the* Pendleton *rescue as the greatest small boat rescue in its history.*

Captain Webster's planning committee carefully mapped out what would happen during the two days of the Cape reunion of Webber's crew. I was part of that planning committee. Among the highlights: a dinner the night before, a luncheon at Chatham Station, a ride aboard the *36500*, group pictures, a cake-cutting ceremony and a tour of the lighthouse at Station Chatham. Through all the fuss, Webber never took his eyes off "his crew." Even after fifty years, Bernie was as protective of Andy, Richard and Ervin as he was aboard the famous *CG36500* that night. And we were all conscious of the stress any reunion would have on the crew, and though the rescue occurred five decades before, some aftershocks of that night still played out in some of their lives.

"For almost fifty years, they had focused on the loss of Tiny Myers, the one *Pendleton* crew [member] who they could not have saved as opposed to the thirty-two they had brought to safety. Long before Post Traumatic Stress Disorder was established as a diagnosis, the crew of *CG36500* experienced personal night terrors from the night of the rescue," reminded Captain Webster. "The reunion brought them back together again with their families and friends and properly acknowledged their heroics and allowed them to privately express the shame they bore in losing Tiny."

It was that weekend when I got the idea to write a book about Bernie's crew. Several years later, *The Pendleton Disaster Off Cape Cod: The Greatest Small Boat Rescue in Coast Guard History* was launched, and I eventually co-authored it first with historian John J. Galluzzo and later, for the second and third editions, with Captain Webster.

From there, we began the Pendleton Leadership Lecture Series along with retired master chief Jack Downey, from whom Captain Webster conceived the reunion idea following that pinning ceremony at Station Chatham. We've been going strong with the series since 2009 and have relayed

Webber's story aboard the *36500* to thousands of emerging young leaders at the Coast Guard Academy; the Leadership Development Center at the Coast Guard Academy; SUNY Maritime in the Bronx; the U.S. Merchant Marine Academy in Kings Point, New York; the Massachusetts Maritime Academy; the Maine Maritime Academy; Norwich University; and the Naval Academy Preparatory School in Newport.

Looking back through a calm lens of reflection, the 2002 reunion was the right thing to do, and it reminded the Coast Guard that key rescues of its service deserved continued recognition and remembrance. Our close friendship with Bernie continued through the years since the '02 reunion, until that day in January 2009 when I picked up a phone message from Captain Webster. "Bernie has passed," he said, and I was shocked beyond anything to hear that. We had just communicated with him a few days prior to his death.

Bernie's family planned his memorial service for early May 2009. Commandant Admiral Thad Allen attended, along with the highest-ranking enlisted noncommissioned officer, Master Chief Skip Bowen. On the return flight to Washington, both men decided that the new series of rescue cutters the Coast Guard was designing would carry the names of enlisted heroes. The first off the production line was the *Bernard C. Webber*, launched with much fanfare in Miami in May 2012. The top reason Admiral Allen was triggered to do this was because he attended Bernie's funeral service.

Captain Webster remembered:

> *I think the Coast Guard leadership, traditionally driven by cuttermen, was just coming to appreciate some things that Bernie Webber and other shore rescue station enlisted men knew—we stand on the shoulders that have come before us. I can't pin it on any particular Commandant or E-10 or even say that Admiral Allen and Master Chief Bowen were the first to "get it," but I know there was a beginning of a focus on history, heritage and acknowledging the role of enlisted heroes a few years before I left the Coast Guard. That doesn't come from any single generation of leaders, I know. But, today, I believe the Coast Guard is on its way to institutionalizing the value of its past successes (and failures) and moving its history program forward with a new museum in New London, Connecticut. The crown jewel in that effort will be when those history lessons learned become part of everyday operational planning so that we never have to relearn our worst mistakes.*

Seth Ellis (second from left) was the sole survivor of the Monomoy Disaster in March 1902. *Courtesy of the W.B. Nickerson Archives, Cape Cod Community College.*

After that fateful rescue mission of 1952, Webber and his crew never got over the loss of Tiny Myers, the one man they couldn't save, even though thirty-two other sailors were rescued. Even at their 2002 reunion in Boston, Bernie, Richard, Ervin and Andy continued to talk about Tiny, the only *Pendleton* crewman they lost that night in '52.

The forerunner to the U.S. Coast Guard was the U.S. Life-Saving Service, founded in 1848. It eventually evolved into the Coast Guard in 1915. Like the Coast Guard, the Life-Saving Service was filled with heroes. One individual in particular was Seth Ellis, the number one surfman at the Monomoy Life-Saving Station.

On March 17, 1902, Ellis was one of eight crewmen who tried to rescue five survivors off a barge named the *Wadena*. The *Wadena* was en route from Newport News, Virginia, for Boston and was traveling in tandem with another barge called the *John C. Fitzpatrick* on March 11. Both barges were towing a tug called *Sweepstakes* when all three vessels ran aground at the southern edge of Monomoy Island, which is located on the Cape's elbow near Chatham. For days, workers attempted to lighten the load of the barges so they could eventually be floated and freed from the sandbar. During this period, barge crewmen were off and on the vessels trying to use daylight hours to free the two barges and the tug.

Most of the crew members from both barges were safely ashore, but on March 17, five individuals said to be recovering personal items remained on the *Wadena*: owner W.S. Mack of Cleveland, Ohio; Captain C.D. Olsen of Boston; and three Portuguese crewmen. After Seth Ellis's boss saw a distress flag on the *Wadena*, however, Ellis, the number one surfman at Monomoy's Life-Saving Station, was ordered to lead a crew to rescue them. Once the five survivors were aboard, waves continued to rock the life-saving boat, and the *Wadena* crewmen clung to the rescuers, leaving them unable to row or steady the boat. After they slipped one by one to their deaths, the only survivor was Seth Ellis, who rarely talked about the rescue in his later years. The failed mission would be known as the Monomoy Disaster because that's exactly what it was.

During the 1952 *Pendleton* rescue, all thirty-two survivors who flooded into the *CG36500* were calm, took directions well and listened to instructions from Bernie and his crew. Their ability to form an instant community in which all members listened to their rescuers probably had a lot to do with the fact that the *Pendleton* crewmen survived. This was clearly not the case with the *Wadena* survivors.

Off the Rails

Wearing white silk with lace sleeves and lily of the valley in her hair, Miss Annie Bearse Lytton Bacon married Lawrence Dexter Hinckley at the Baptist church in Hyannis on Thursday, June 11, 1908. Following a fancy reception at the home of her parents, the *Hyannis Patriot* newspaper reported that the newlyweds "took the afternoon train to Boston, Salem and vicinity."

Several years later, Eva Hooper Clark wed Albert Whiting Doolittle in January 1912 at her parents' home in Sandwich. "The bride was beautifully gowned in white satin messaline, trimmed with Point de Venise lace. She wore a veil fastened with lilies of the valley and carried a bouquet of white roses and lilies of the valley," said the *Barnstable Patriot* in its January 1912 edition. After the bride and groom made a quick getaway in a borrowed auto, "parties went to Sagamore and Buzzards Bay and others took the train to Boston, hoping to overtake the couple."

Aside from donning similar wedding dresses and the playing of Lohengrin's ubiquitous "Wedding March" at the services, each couple had something in common: the railroad on Cape Cod was a part of their wedding plans.

In a larger perspective, often hidden in the story of the rails, which were designed to close the gap in rail service between Middleborough and Wareham, are the changes this momentous technology wrought on local culture.

From the moment the nearly fifteen-mile inaugural segment between Wareham and Middleborough opened for business on January 26, 1848, with nearly fifteen miles of track, Cape Cod was changed forever in several ways.

Completed in 1892, this depot at Gray Gables in the town of Bourne was built to accommodate President Grover Cleveland's nearby residence, the so-called first White House on Cape Cod. *Courtesy of the Phil Choate Collection, courtesy of Bill Reidy.*

First off, for the first time, Cape Codders had to tell time, to the minute. Before January 26, 1848, folks might have been a few minutes late to a church service, or school or to open their businesses. But rail service, as convenient as it was, also delivered a time-accountability to a whole population for the first time in nineteenth-century life on Cape Cod. "Cape Codders who traveled via stagecoach did have to be aware of the time before the railroad arrived, but it was likely a limited part of the population that frequently used the stages," explained Bill Reidy of the Cape Cod Chapter of the National Railroad Historical Society. He added that travel was now an option for most Cape Codders, who could take the train up to Boston, spend a few hours and then return by day's end. Before, travel off Cape was a lengthy process via packet boat, horseback or stagecoach.

Secondly, access to a railroad meant that Cape Cod was no longer off anyone's beaten path. Outsiders could come here at virtually any time, and this was a huge deal since Cape Codders preferred to keep to themselves. But apparently along the way, a silent tradeoff had been reached: privacy for convenience. Later that year, in May 1848, nearly thirteen additional miles of track connected Wareham to Sandwich. Now it was possible to travel between Sandwich and Boston. More rail tracks were added in 1853 so a line could connect to Hyannis, and by December 22, 1853, service had begun in West Barnstable.

The West Barnstable Railroad Station was constructed in 1911. *Courtesy of the Cape Cod Chapter of the National Railroad Historical Society.*

The Hyannis Railroad Station was completed in 1854. *Courtesy of the Bill Reidy Collection.*

In early 1854, the Cape Cod Branch Railroad was rechristened the Cape Cod Railroad Company. Rail service had reached the mid-Cape, and train whistles were heard in Barnstable village on May 8, 1854, and

Constructed of granite walls and stretching one thousand feet, the old railroad wharf in Hyannis Port was completed in 1854. Steamships docked at its end. *Courtesy of the Bill Reidy Collection.*

in Yarmouth Port on May 19, 1854, and finally in the bustling village of Hyannis on July 8, 1854.

And thirdly, the advent of rail service now meant that hip commuters and tourists could take a ferry from Nantucket and hop a train in Hyannis, bound for Boston. How very trendy that was in 1854.

This service would continue until 1872, when steamboat service for Nantucket was transferred to the new Woods Hole terminal.

The Cape Cod Railroad in 1868 had subsumed the Cape Cod Central Railroad that operated a line from Orleans to Yarmouth since 1865. (Problem was, this straight shot between Yarmouth to Orleans skipped right by Chatham.) And the owners of the rail line didn't stop there; they kept buying up stretches of independently owned track. The Cape Cod Railroad purchased the Plymouth and Vineyard Sound Railroad in 1871, but it wasn't until 1872 that operations kicked off in Woods Hole.

In time, the Cape Cod Railroad outgrew its own boots through a merger with the Old Colony and Newport Railway to form the aptly renamed Old Colony Railroad. Headquartered in Hyannis, the Cape Cod rail sections went by a new name: the Cape Cod Division. And finally, in July 1873, rail service had stretched all the way to Provincetown. "At Provincetown, the railroad ended on a long wharf out into the harbor," explained Bill Reidy. "Unlike Hyannis and Woods Hole, however, the railroad never ran regularly scheduled passenger service out onto the wharf to meet ferries or other ships.

Rail service atop a wharf in Provincetown, circa 1911. *Courtesy of the Bill Reidy Collection.*

Passenger trains terminated at Provincetown Station by Bradford Street"
near MacMillan Wharf, said Reidy.

All told, there were forty-eight train stops in every Cape Cod town
except Mashpee.

Another untold dynamic to all this progress was the toll taken on the
landscape of Cape Cod. Picture a giant knife dug into the spine of the
Cape, between Route 28 to the south and Route 6A to the north. All those
trees, through wetlands and farms and private property, were all uprooted,
drained and trampled on in the name of a railroad. Today, however, I can
thoroughly enjoy the same terrain as the old railroad tracks because the bike
trail, the Cape Cod Rail Trail, runs atop the old track lanes.

Chatham was the last town to get its own depot, and did it wait a long
time for rail service! "Finally in the mid-1880s, townspeople got together and
financed construction of the standard-gauge Chatham Railroad Company
branch from Harwich, to be operated by the Old Colony Railroad," recounted
Reidy. The line was opened on November 21, 1887. "The new rail line
elevated Chatham to a favored summertime tourist destination, along with
the other Cape towns with railroad service. It also greatly benefited the town's
businesses, particularly those related to the fishing industry," Reidy added.

Over time, even the innovative rail system on Cape Cod underwent a
transformation. In 1959, the New Haven Railroad stopped its service to
key depots in southeastern Massachusetts, including Plymouth, Scituate,

Middleboro and Cape Cod. "The key driver here was the railroad losing a tremendous amount of money on its commuter operations to local communities outside of Boston and New York City," clarified Reidy. "It was still making money on its longer-distance trains, such as the summertime trains from Boston and New York City to the Cape. Much of this was due to the construction of taxpayer-subsidized highways paralleling the New Haven routes, while the railroad was required to maintain its right of ways and pay real estate taxes for the privilege to boot," Reidy said. In 1947, the New Haven line won the legal right to abandon its Old Colony line commuter services out of Boston based on a previous bankruptcy reorganization dating to the Great Depression years. But it wasn't until June 30, 1959, that the entity exercised its right to do so. However, summertime rail service continued through 1964, with the exception of 1959.

As is often the case in Cape Cod history, the adage "what goes around, comes around" is true. Aristotle said, "Past is prologue." Today, rail service continues, at least in Hyannis, through two stations, as noted by Bill Reidy: "The Cape Cod Central's depot [is] at 252 Main Street, the site of Hyannis' original railroad station, while the Hyannis Transportation Center at 215 Iyannough Road is home to the seasonal Boston-Hyannis Cape*FLYER* service."

In the Loony Bin

It's a unique sound in nature, one that Native Americans have called "the Cry of the Earth." It's the distinctive sound that has inspired poets and naturalists, not to mention a score of scientists over the generations. And it's a wild cry that most people think is heard only on freshwater lakes in the northern woods of New England. But here on Cape Cod, hidden no more, common loons (*Gavia immer*) "winter over" on salt water, and their unique yodels and tremolos share space with the cold air. They are spotted along beaches, including the entry channel into Great Sippewissett Marsh in West Falmouth, in Osterville and on Chatham's South Beach.

Some liken the haunting song of the loon to the soprano of a wolf call, and these variable voices are most vocal from mid-May to mid-July in the wilds of Maine, New Hampshire and Vermont, as well as the upper Midwest, the Northwest and into Canada. Loons sing four distinct calls, and each signifies a specific communication. The tremolo, known as the "crazy laugh," signals alarm and is usually sung out at night to advertise its territory. But it's the wail call that sounds like a wolf's howl, and it can be heard during social interactions, including mating and in answer to other loon tremolos. Only males yodel: a long, rising call lasting six seconds using repetitive notes. It's these cries that startle unknowing Cape Codders because most of us don't think loons are here—hence their hidden value to the natural scene.

On your average visit to Cape Cod, "few things are more hidden from casual observers than the large numbers of wintering seabirds. Mostly gray or black and white, the many species present blend into the pewter-

Common loons *(Gavia immer)* claim one of the most haunting calls in nature. *Courtesy of Emily Eaton.*

colored seascape," according to Mark Pokras, DVM, of Tufts University. "The uninitiated may think they are all ducks at a distance out there beyond the waves. But if you take the time to look, there are grebes, auks, murres, eiders, mergansers, loons and other birds that come to feed in the rich waters around Cape Cod," Pokras added. In truth, loons embody the primal mysteriousness of nature.

There's a whole other universe over our heads, and Cape Cod's hidden value to the natural world rests in a geographic capacity. The entire Outer Cape is beneath an "outer coast" flyway used for eons by migratory birds. In fact, the 7,604-acre Monomoy National Wildlife Refuge, which was established in 1944, is a critical migratory stop for birds using this global flyway. This same area became a Western Hemisphere Shorebird Reserve Network (WHSRN) regional site in 1999. It's important to think about Cape Cod as more than a summer stop for tourists; it has its importance in the natural world as well. "When I say common loons, people are often surprised because they're not seeing the regal black and white birds with the bright red eyes and the mysterious wailing calls that they saw in the movie *On Golden Pond* or have experienced on northern lakes," noted Pokras. "But winter loons are much more subtle. Mottled gray above and light below, their eyes turned gray-brown, our winter loons glide silently along our coastal waters feeding on fish and crabs. So when you're walking winter beaches on the Cape, you may not be seeing loons. But I guarantee that loons are watching you," he said.

Noted wildlife photographer and author Heather E. Fone of Centerville, who's also a licensed wildlife rehabilitator and educator at Massachusetts Audubon's Long Pasture Sanctuary, was surprised one December morning by a sighting of common loons. "The entrance to Dowses Beach in Osterville has an inlet [on] either side of the road before you reach the beach area, and as I drove in on a particularly cold morning I was surprised to see not one or two common loons but six swimming together!"

Loons are water birds that live in both fresh and salt water. They are seen all over the Cape in winter and just offshore from September to May prior to heading back up north for the nesting season. The penguin is their closest living relative. (Odd, for sure, but not so much in the natural world if you consider that hippopotami are the closest living relative to cetaceans [whales].)

Unless you're a serious "birder," most people equate and limit avian diversity on Cape Cod to seagulls, robins, blue jays and water fowl like ducks and geese. But loons are here, just not year-round.

"It was quite a sight, and even though the loons were in their winter plumage and not the beautiful black and white summer plumage, it was a thrill to see so many together," recounted Fone.

It's a Shell Life

From the farmer's table to restaurants with crisp, white tabletops, in the nineteenth century turtles were prized as a key ingredient in soup and other culinary delicacies throughout Barnstable County. These days, how times have changed. Any reasonable Cape Codder wouldn't dream of eating them, and indeed, the race is on to conserve this charismatic reptile.

Nina Coleman is the Sandy Neck park manager in the Town of Barnstable's Marine and Environmental Affairs Department. Sandy Neck equals 4,700 acres and at times feels like one big sand dune as you trudge up and down its dynamic and shifting hills to step into thatches of wild beach grasses and low-lying indigenous plants and shrubs. It hasn't changed much at all through the centuries. It remains a cool mix of yesteryear and contemporary, with its fifty private cottages—many of them antiques—mixed in among the dunes. Sandy Neck's official clarification is that of a barrier beach and an Area of Critical Environmental Concern (ACEC), so designated by the Commonwealth of Massachusetts. A lifeguarded beach open to the public is among the treasures of Sandy Neck.

But it's the living creatures that make this place special, endangered species like piping plovers, terns, spadefoot toads and the northeastern diamondback terrapins. It's these turtles that occupy Nina Coleman's waking hours.

"Every year on Sandy Neck Beach, a small percentage of diamondback terrapins nest on sandy roads where their eggs are in danger of being crushed by vehicles. These eggs will likely not survive without intervention," explains Coleman. Her team carefully removes the eggs from these roadways, places

A diamondback terrapin hatchling. *Courtesy of Sean Kortis.*

them in incubators and raises the hatchlings over the winter or, as we say on Cape Cod, "over winter." Many schools have taken these baby turtles, which spend the winters in glass aquariums in select classrooms in Barnstable and Sandwich. "The turtles are then released back into the marsh in the spring," Coleman adds, when they have grown and have a better chance at surviving. This process is called "headstarting."

Terrapins are protected under the Massachusetts Endangered Species Act and are currently listed as "threatened." "Headstarting allows the hatchlings to grow to the size of a two- to three-year-old wild juvenile terrapin in just six months," claims Coleman, and this greatly increases survivorship rates.

After a long winter, the students take a field trip to Sandy Neck Beach, where, with much fanfare, these juveniles are released into the Great Marsh instead of taking a short trip to the cooking pot. What a difference a mere century can make!

The Beloved Beacon

On October 1, 1826, Joseph Nickerson reported to work as the first keeper at Sandy Neck Light, which guarded the eastern sector of Barnstable Harbor on the dynamic and restless shoreline that spanned six miles in length and only a half mile in width. Nickerson earned $350 a year and lived on-site in the keeper's six-room house. Featuring ten lamps boasting the power of 180 candles and said to be visible for nine nautical miles, Sandy Neck Light kept watch over a bustling maritime trade that included coastal schooners, fishing vessels and whaling boats.

Winters were merciless along that sandy spit. Nickerson's successor, Henry Baxter, wrote in his records on December 15, 1834, "This day a heavy gale from the SW with snow. Came on shore the schooner *Enterprise*…and Capt. Sawyer with two women on board. Got them on shore with much trouble. Capt. Sawyer much frost bite. So ends very cold and the ice making fast the schooner, laying in the barr [*sic*] with much ice on her and sails much torn."

In the years ahead, Harry Baxter's son, James, and another Baxter, Thomas P.D. Baxter, also served as keeper at Sandy Neck, as would Jacob S. Howes and George A. Jamieson in the decades ahead.

But what's often hidden about this iconic light is that two widows also served in the arduous role as keeper after their husbands passed away while on the job. Even on nineteenth-century Cape Cod, with its quintessential ideals about how women should be dainty and not have to lift anything heavy, these women—Lucy Hinckley Baxter and, later, Eunice Crowell Howes—broke the proverbial mold.

Sandy Neck, one of the most iconic lighthouses on Cape Cod, once employed no fewer than two female keepers. *Courtesy of Sturgis Library.*

In the grueling winter of 1862, Thomas P.D. Baxter was rowing his dory to Barnstable through an ice-laden harbor when his leg was crushed between the boat and a thick chunk of ice. This led to gangrene and a painful death. Lucy assumed Thomas's job and kept at it until 1867. Her grandson Harry Ryder relayed to historian Edward Rowe Snow the following anecdote: "The picture she often described to us of having to heat the whale oil in the winter months behind the kitchen stove and carry two oil butts up into the tower at midnight is one we never forget."

In 1875, Jacob S. Howes became keeper at Sandy Neck, but he passed on in 1880. Like Lucy had done before her, his widow, Eunice, assumed his keeper position until 1886. The same year Howes died, the keeper's house, about fifty-four years old by this time, appeared beyond repair, and a new one was constructed, the same structure that's there today.

By 1931, the need for Sandy Neck Light had decreased to a degree that the federal government recommended decommission, sending the iconic facility into surplus mode. "It was taken out of use in 1931 due to Barnstable Harbor's decreasing importance as well as the fact that the shifting sands of Sandy Neck moved the lighthouse further from the outer coast of the beach," wrote Chris Setterlund. "Two years later the lantern was taken off, leaving the lighthouse 'headless' until it was restored to its full working order with a new lantern in 2007," he added.

A series of purchases by private hands followed the 1931 federal furlough, first to Warren J. Clear in 1933 for $711 and then to Francis and Margaret Ellis. For a time, the Coast Guard leased Sandy Neck from the Ellises during World War II, until radio personality Fred Lang purchased it in 1944. From Lang, ownership of Sandy Neck went to the Hinckley family; today, Sandy Neck is managed by Ken Morton and his mother, Elizabeth Hinckley "Skee" Morton, under the auspices of a family trust.

The grand lady may have changed her dress—or shingles—over the years, but the grace and dignity remain intact at Sandy Neck Light, even if her beacon doesn't shine for the safety of mariners.

That Writer, Margaret

The small book, a literary classic, sat on my nightstand so long that it began to gather dust, which was swept away during weekly cleanings. Then I foolishly and thoughtlessly put it back on a shelf in my library. "I'll read it later," I told myself—until the moment I saw a picture of the book's author, and then I knew I had to read the book straightaway.

Here's what happened: I had been rummaging through a box of images at the William Brewster Nickerson Cape Cod History Archives at Cape Cod Community College, trying to scope out hidden history for this book, when I came across an image of Margaret A. Stanger. "I know that name," I thought. Then it clicked.

That Quail, Robert, is her work, and that's the book, first published in 1966, that sat on my nightstand for months. It's the true story of a little bird that preferred human companionship rather than the company of its own kind. In its day, this humble book about a bird on Cape Cod became a national bestseller. For a long while, Margaret Stanger's contribution to Cape Cod's literary scene was tantamount to what Mark Twain's means to the Mississippi River or Willa Cather's on the Great Plains.

Aside from its locale on our wonderful Cape Cod, *That Quail, Robert,* awakened in readers fresh knowledge that animals were distinct and individual, emotion-bearing beings, a movement of thought that was gaining momentum in the 1960s, when this book was first published.

"Along with *Born Free* and *Rascal,* this true story of the little quail that loved people ranks among the great nature tales of all time," opined the *Boston Globe.*

Margaret Stanger of Orleans composed a literary classic about a quail that lived with humans. *Courtesy of the W.B. Nickerson Archives, Cape Cod Community College.*

And to think, Stanger was born in Falmouth and later lived in Orleans. In truth, the Cape is filled with established and important writers: the poet Mary Oliver of Provincetown and acclaimed military historian Carlo D'Este of Marstons Mills, among many others. But Stanger's book came aligned with the emerging trend of animal rights and awareness of wild creatures, which makes her work all the more seminal. Yet in these times, it is quietly hidden on a library shelf.

Stanger was smart and accomplished. Her BA was from Grinnell College, and she holds an MA from Columbia University. A nurse by trade and a born nurturer, Margaret retired to the Cape to four wooded acres on Crystal Lake, and through her friends and neighbors, Dr. Thomas Kienzle and his wife, Mildred, was introduced to a hatchling they named Robert in July 1962. The Kienzles found a perfect little egg in an abandoned quail nest in their yard and brought it indoors, where it hatched three days later. "There emerged slowly something resembling a wet bumblebee in size and general appearance," Stanger wrote. Even though she wasn't a trained writer, Stanger's heartfelt composition belies an eloquent and engaging dialogue with a reader: "Even then, at the puffball stage, he was really beautiful, with muted shadings in his coloring, lighter on the breast than on the back, and with very bright little eyes."

At the tender age of three weeks, the Kienzles took Robert outside for the first time and placed him on the ground. Setting him free, they thought, was the right thing to do. "The reaction was unexpected. He looked around in bewilderment for a minute or two, then with excited little calls he began scratching, biting off tender tips of grass, and almost immediately he spied a tiny bug, which he ran after and ate." When they walked back toward the house, Robert followed, and from then on, he refused to stay outdoors.

Robert had become part of the family. Every day, Robert checked the baseboards for spiders, and if he found one, he ate it. "If Mildred was sewing in the sewing room, Robert was there, investigating patterns, running off with bits of cloth and generally participating in the project. If Tommy was reading the paper, Robert was in his lap, begging for attention." (As a side note, after Robert laid an egg, he became known as a she.)

So begins a wondrous journey in Robert's life on Cape Cod that remains a classic in American literature.

That Quail, Robert, is a quick read. Indeed, I made a pot of tea, picked up the book, read it in an hour, and the last of the tea hadn't even gone cold yet. But it's an engrossing, humane treatment of a human, functional relationship with a wild creature, albeit with an expected bittersweet ending. These days I don't hear much about the book. Still, this timeless treasure claims Cape Cod as its home, even though it's largely hidden to current generations.

Cape Cod's Little Italy

Along Hanover Street in Boston's North End, there is no end to culinary options, with dozens of renowned restaurants and smaller mom-and-pop places, even on those side streets. It's the same thing on Federal Hill in Providence, where Italians set up shop, literally, several generations ago.

Cape Cod's very own Little Italy in Buzzards Bay, a village of Bourne, was "incorporated" in 1937, when Speranza Cubellis and her husband from Woonsocket, Rhode Island, visited Cape Cod and liked what they saw. They decided to open first a food stand that served spaghetti and sauce and then a boardinghouse, which evolved into a restaurant she named Mezza Luna, which means "half moon" in Italian.

Speranza passed on in 1980 at the ripe age of ninety, but her grandson, Emilio John "E.J." Cubellis II, remembers his cherished "Nona," especially her tremendous and inspiring work habits. Speaking from his kitchen at the famed Main Street eatery, E.J. said, "If she didn't work twelve, fourteen, sixteen hours a day, she didn't know what to do with herself," and this was during her retirement years! To please his mother, E.J.'s father built her a "little store" called Mama's Pizzeria. "She had a little deli and made her homemade bread every day," he recounted. "She used to sleep in the boiler room because it was warm," Cubellis said.

Speranza, who was born in Naples, Italy, and immigrated to America, would wake up every morning at 4:00 a.m. to start the bread. "Then she

Speranza Cubellis (center), founder of Mezza Luna, inaugurated Cape Cod's "Little Italy" in Buzzards Bay. *Courtesy of E.J. Cubellis.*

would sell to people all day long." Rarely out of the kitchen, E.J. said his Nona "had an apron on for most of her life."

Mezza Luna is an Upper Cape institution. Back in the 1950s and '60s, says Cubellis, families would come into his Nona's store and buy a loaf of her homemade bread and a pound each of salami, prosciutto and provolone cheese and then make sandwiches in their cars as they traveled down Cape Cod roadways during vacations and short sightseeing tours. All that food "for just six or seven dollars," Cubellis added.

It's a business that's been tried and tested. On October 20, 2007, a suspected electrical fire gutted the Buzzards Bay landmark, and it wasn't until April 6, 2009, that Mezza Luna reopened to much fanfare.

Cubellis, forty-two, has worked at Mezza Luna all his life and took over its management and co-ownership in 1992. Two daughters and a son of Speranza have survived their mother; two other sons, including E.J.'s father, have passed on. But as a kid, he got off the school bus "and came here." His late father gave him the job of "stirring the sauce" while standing on a milk carton in order to reach the stovetop.

What's his secret to business success?

The food is "simple and authentic," even the meals and snacks Speranza prepared for E.J. "I loved the fried dough," he remembered. Nona would wrap the dough with sugar in a bag or slit it open and "put butter on it. The best warm toast you could have in your life."

A Hidden Century

Historians and journalists unearth stories in both obvious and odd ways. In some cases, happily, a story falls into one's lap. When standing in the basement of the Falmouth Historical Society researching the history of servants on Cape Cod, I happened to ask curator Amanda Wastrom what she thought a hidden gem of history might be. Her response was swift. "All of the twentieth century," she replied. I was so astounded and subsequently interested that I merely egged her on for more and asked her why. "It's because ever since the Cape was created as a tourist destination in the late 1800s, the whole concept of the Cape was to come to a colonial or pre-colonial region, and so there's been deliberate work to market this area as that, and I think things that don't quite fit into that narrative tend to get pushed to the side," Wastrom clarified.

Well, I thought to myself, if all of the twentieth century itself is a hidden gem in Cape Cod's history, then the unveiling of the knowing and understanding that fact now isn't.

Here's a prime example: World War II and the critical involvement in that conflict by the town of Falmouth. When people think of war and Cape Cod, what usually comes to mind? The Revolutionary War, of course, or for purists, the War of 1812. Both conflicts share the British persecution of Cape Cod's waters, but those tales have been told time and time again. The tremendous lift to Falmouth's economy because of World War II has rarely been examined.

World War II transformed the town of Falmouth from a sleepy tourist outpost to a military staging area when the federal government threw its

This undated image from the Massachusetts Military Reservation reveals a heavily used training site. *Courtesy of the W.B. Nickerson Archives, Cape Cod Community College.*

resources behind a steep upgrade of Camp Edwards in September 1940. According to Clark Craig, who reported for *Harper's Magazine*'s March 1941 edition, on September 16, 1940, 370 mobile units of the 68th Regiment conveyed into Falmouth toward Camp Edwards, looming formidable with their six-wheeled lorries on which fifty-millimeter anti-aircraft guns were stocked. The regiment made camp on the military reservation, while the 211th Regiment Coast Artillery, Battery G, of the Massachusetts National Guard, made up mostly of men from Falmouth, made camp in the town itself. For a time, before they left for Camp Hulen in Texas for twelve months of training, the soldiers lived on the second floor of the town hall.

And it was here that Falmouth's military past met its present in a series of actions in which the country began preparing for war even before the United States formally entered World War II.

"For several days the townspeople were treated to the sight of their sons drilling beside a monument bearing the names of Falmouth men who died in World War Number One and erected on the very ground where

Minute Men, ancestors of more than one of the present soldiers, drilled in preparation for service at Cambridge and Ticonderoga. During both the Revolution and the War of 1812 cannon balls from attacking British warships had crashed through Falmouth houses and bounced off the same training grounds," Craig noted.

The socioeconomics of Falmouth and, to a lesser degree, three towns that also touched the Massachusetts Military Reservation, were altered forever because the federal government announced it needed dozens of contracts filled in order to build a huge training facility at Camp Edwards. The work had to be finished within seventy-five days "to accommodate the new draft army," wrote Craig. Up to 1,400 buildings, a sewage treatment plant, a hospital, a railroad junction, barracks, offices, a post office, streets and roadways—basically an entire new town—all were necessary within the boundaries of the twenty-four-square-mile reservation. That reservation in those days occupied parts of Bourne, Falmouth, Mashpee and Sandwich.

The Walsh Construction Company won the bid, and "overnight, materials, officials, and workmen began pouring into Camp Edwards and overflowing into the surrounding towns," Craig recounted. Laborers earned $0.62 an hour, while carpenters were paid just over $1.00 per hour. All told, over twenty-thousand men were eventually hired, and the weekly payroll exceeded $750,000. "Never in all history had such a deluge throbbed through the economic arteries of Cape Cod," mused Craig. Still, this equaled good and bad news for town neighboring Camp Edwards.

Clearly, demand overwhelmed supply. "Hardware stores were stripped of tools immediately and couldn't get orders filled fast enough…restaurants had to begin serving breakfasts and preparing lunches at five o'clock in the morning to get all the men to Camp on time," recounted Craig. These extra workers were housed in private homes that became boardinghouses overnight, earning owners more money than they'd ever seen. Reported Craig: "For a three-month period upwards of 300 families took in between 12 and 15 thousand dollars a week in board and room rent…Retail trade in the town was running almost 100 per cent [sic] above seasonal normal."

A global war had transformed a small Cape Cod town in a matter of mere days. The last physical vestige of World War II was a building that was constructed as a service club for soldiers, according to writer Frederick Turkington. Until it was replaced around 1988, locals still referred to it as the old USO club.

I also asked Amanda, if it's true that so much has changed in Cape Cod's recorded history these past several hundred years, what then remains the same? Wastrom answered, "Cape Codders have been ambivalent about tourists, and that's still true today." How right she is. Ask any year-round resident how much they dread Memorial Day Weekend, which is the traditional kickoff of the summer season, and they'll probably roll their eyes at you, thinking of the traffic snarls in rotaries, for example. Then again, business owners who depend on tourists can't wait for that time of year when profits are at their highest.

Continuing along the "what remains the same" theme is what Amanda calls the "continuum of issues." Pressing issues for Cape Codders over the course of numerous generations remain the same today as in yesteryear. "People were arguing about what to do with our natural resources in the 1600s and 1700s," notes Wastrom, adding, "People have been struggling with these issues since colonial times."

Keepers of the Keys

One by one, many have left us, but fortunately some treasures remain here today. They were our friends, colleagues, mentors and teachers. In some way or form, in small or great ways, they helped shape the contemporary dialogue of historic preservation on Cape Cod. If professional academics who hold doctorate degrees in history and teach at universities and colleges normally focus on larger regional trends, events and issues, the people who run the historical societies in each of the Cape's fifteen towns—and the smaller societies representing villages in those towns—deserve our attention, thanks and gratitude because their work is infinitely hyper-focused on one geographic area or town. And a lot of data and research on this micro-level occurs, all of which adds to and complements the canon of exploration that professional historians and academics need for their own work.

Historical societies on Cape Cod are composed of a small legion of amateur and professional historians and docents who have spent countless years in "chronicle mode" to capture and honor Cape Cod history. Without their contributions, we simply wouldn't know as much as we do, wouldn't have as many artifacts as we have and wouldn't be able to continue the work of preserving and honoring our collective heritage.

The sheer number of items that have been donated or acquired by Cape Cod historical societies could indeed fill a big-city museum. But therein lies an inherent and collective concern. Amanda Wastrom, curator at the Falmouth Historical Society, said it best: "We have tons of stuff, and often times the stories behind the objects are lost. And so we have these amazing objects, and as an artist I'm interested in these, but we've lost the stories behind them." Often, donations made long ago came without paper detailing their precise provenance, name or donor or the story behind, for example, a piece of period clothing or a beautifully preserved porcelain doll.

For someone like myself—someone who lives and dies via words—I speak for many historians who rely on these societies for content, guidance and support. No writer of historical topics goes it alone, and those who say they do may be stretching the truth. Simply, it doesn't happen. People with knowledge depend on one another, and information travels and is shared between research facilities, university archives and community entities one generous pair of hands at a time.

Fortunately, I knew them and called them my friends, and I keenly recognize that I have been the beneficiary of their generosity, and my work in history has been complemented by their kindness and knowledge. Here are a few hidden yarns about people who have helped to shape Cape Cod history, quietly and without fanfare.

Many people have been an indispensible part of my journey in writing about the past, but their own journeys remain largely hidden from the much wider audiences they deserve. Here are a few of their stories.

In late March 1990, I had been married for a year and was heavily pregnant with our first child; Katherine Margaret would arrive on April 24, 1990. Although by then I had been a television, radio and print news reporter for ten years, several months earlier I had taken the leap into the past and started composing historical vignettes on a freelance basis for the *Yarmouth Register*, a weekly newspaper begun in 1836. I never wanted to see the inside of a newsroom again, I told myself, so working freelance now felt right.

My editor at the time, Dana Hornig, a nice guy but intimidatingly no-nonsense, suggested I profile Margaret Milliken, a retired teacher who used to also write historical stories about Yarmouth. I followed Dana's lead and contacted Margaret. She wasn't what I expected as I waddled through her front door and was thankfully shown to a comfy chair. I had expected someone much younger; when we met, Margaret was clearly north of eighty. But she was bright as a new penny, and Margaret later confided that she "felt as if I was twenty."

Within minutes of meeting me for the first time, Margaret deftly maneuvered her walker as she poured tea and started to talk about the past. Little did I know then that our ritual of afternoon tea had begun, and I would continue to visit her in the coming years. She taught me many things.

As a young girl, she was an eyewitness to the suffragette movement; she lived at Windsor Castle in England in the 1950s during a period of study as an organist; and she lived through the Roaring Twenties, the Depression and two world wars. Her anecdotes on local and regional history were extremely helpful in my early years of research and writing.

And she made a mean tea, and I don't mean from teabags. Margaret was a purist and always added hot tap water to a teapot to prep for loose tea. She said she learned how to make proper tea while living in England during her younger years. "Stir it seven times clockwise, and seven times counter-clockwise," she taught me, and to this day I do. Margaret also baked. How she did this with a walker, I do not know. Her specialties were Parker House rolls, which she served with jam, and Nutmeg Feather Cake, which was otherworldly. Margaret is no longer living, but her works of local history continue to educate and entertain.

One day, Margaret and I were having tea when Priscilla Gregory walked in to drop off something to Margaret. Priscilla was vice-president of the Historical Society of Old Yarmouth (HSOY) in the early 1990s and a member of the Yarmouth Historical Commission. Along with Judy Thomas, Priscilla edited *Yarmouth: Old Homes and Gathering Places*, published by the commission in 1989, and served as the book's principal researcher. It's a seminal inventory of what the title suggests: homes, businesses and gathering places in the town of Yarmouth. I used Priscilla's book often as a reference during my years as a freelancer at the *Register* in the early 1990s. Priscilla was an early inspiration and source of support for my work, a real mentor. Priscilla is still with us today, and no doubt one hundred years from now, a historian not yet born will deeply appreciate her book.

Priscilla introduced me to the Historical Society of Old Yarmouth, which I still think is one of the most functional historical societies on Cape Cod. At any rate, there I met Haynes Mahoney, who sadly passed on in 2014. Haynes was the author of a humble yet thoroughly researched monograph called *Yarmouth's Proud Packets*, published in 1986 by the HSOY. Like Margaret and Priscilla, Haynes was immensely interesting. He spent thirty-four years as a Foreign Service officer with the United States Information Agency and served in Munich, Frankfurt, Bangkok, Tokyo and Berlin, among other places. But he came home to Yarmouth Port and explored his passion of sailing ships in the Great Age of Sail. And Haynes had this enormous curiosity about packet ships, which were schooners that served as "water taxis" carrying people and goods on a fixed route and timetable between Cape Cod, then an island, and the mainland.

Here's a bit from Mahoney's book:

But why Yarmouth packets? After all, the town had only a couple of tidal creeks for harbors on its north shore, and one river, nearly closed by the bar at low tide, for vessels making port in the "South Sea." Surely Barnstable, Provincetown, Hyannis or Falmouth with their deeper harbors, bustled with superior maritime traffic than little Yarmouth. This might be true, but contemporary newspaper accounts and earlier historians disclose that Yarmouth sported the fastest packets on Cape Cod Bay in its boisterous maritime years before the Civil War, and ran busy coasting lines up and down the eastern seaboard out of Bass River, despite its semi-diurnal shallows. As representative of the packet period Yarmouth seems an eminently seaworthy community.

In those early years at HSOY, I met two other individuals who worked closely together and have contributed much to the historical landscape but were as different at chalk and cheese: Jack Braginton-Smith and Duncan Oliver. Jack owned the aptly named Jack's Outback in Yarmouth Port and was considered the dean of history in our village. Jack was famous for insulting people who came into his restaurant. He is alleged to have shouted at people, including admonishing one portly man who ordered French fries.

His personal archives, I'm told, were to be envied, but in truth, he never let anyone upstairs in his apartment, which was located on the second floor of his restaurant. "I'm writing all these books," Jack would say, but he never seemed to actually bring any project to fruition—until he met Duncan. Duncan nudged Jack to transform his scholarship into book form, and the two pooled their intellectual capital. Duncan is a retired history teacher and academic administrator who co-authored two books with Jack, *Port on the Bay: Yarmouth's Maritime History on the "North Sea" 1638 to the Present* and *Cape Cod Shore Whaling: America's First Whalemen.*

Their publications are hardly in every bookstore on Cape Cod, but the university-grade scholarship remains largely hidden from view from wider audiences who would no doubt appreciate the depth and scope of their research. Jack passed on some years ago, but Duncan remains an integral part of the HSOY.

Both men were exceedingly generous with their time. Whenever I needed a historical article, issue or trend clarified, explained or vetted, they served as my go-to sources. The range of scholarship that Duncan still produces for the *Register* is impressive.

In Dennis, one town to the east, two historians were instrumental along my pathway in history. Years ago, I met Phyllis Horton of the Dennis Historical Society. I've known her so long that I can't even remember when we met. Her equally talented daughter, Lynne, teaches history at Dennis-Yarmouth Regional High School. Phyllis is a wealth of knowledge about the town of Dennis. A descendant of mariners and an independent scholar, Phyllis could easily teach a college course in Cape Cod maritime history. One of her many contributions was an article from April 2009 describing three major wharves in Dennis:

> At one time, 400 vessels called Dennis Port their homeport. At that point it was called Crocker's Neck. It became Dennis Port in 1863. But Dennis Port didn't have its own post office. They had to go to West Harwich (one village over) for their mail. Thomas Howes had a general store and he went to West Harwich everyday, and he brought back mail for everyone who shopped with him, and he'd bring back someone else's mail who didn't shop with him. Howes was the one who named Dennis Port. The first post office was in his store.

We are blessed to have Phyllis with us still, and she is quite active in historical research to this day.

Through Phyllis I met the late Burton Derek, a keenly irascible but profoundly generous man whose contributions to Dennis history are unfortunately confined to that town's borders simply because there wasn't widespread interest outside of the community. You know those jokes people make about being smart as a nuclear physicist? Well, Burton was indeed engaged in such a profession. He worked for decades for the DuPont Corporation in plastic fiber optics, traveling the world before he formally retired to his hometown in the late '90s.

I remember a specific story about Burt. I had come across a very sad story about a teenage girl from Dennis in the 1840s and the circumstances of her tragic death that I wanted to include in a column I used to write for the *Cape Cod Voice*, a bimonthly newsmagazine that was in print about ten years ago on the Lower Cape. I knew Burt was familiar with the story that I was researching. "You are not to use her last name," he vehemently cautioned me. "Some of her family are still alive in Dennis today. You release her last name, and you won't get any more research from this town." Of course, I never revealed Elizabeth's last name, and I share this story to convey how deeply protective Burt was about key aspects of his town's history. And yes, I meant to say "his" town. Burt's mother was the late Pauline Wixon Derek, a noted historian and genealogist who died in 1997. Burt's maternal grandfather was Nathaniel H. Wixon, a businessman in Dennis for whom the middle school off Route 134 is named.

As his obituary noted, Burt's contributions to preservation are incalculable. In his role as an archivist for the Dennis Historical Society, he had digitally converted "well over 50,000 pieces of Dennis history," from pictures, log books, letters and journals. And he was immensely generous. I once stood chatting in his dining room along with his wife of forty years, Ruth, when Burt was showing me some of his work. He picked up a thick, blue hardcover book called *Dennis Records Volume 1* and simply said, "Here." To have received such a gift in my line of work was huge, and for that I am eternally grateful.

In terms of generosity and knowledge, Burt's counterpart in the town of Yarmouth has to be Barry Homer of South Yarmouth. There are streets and parks named for people in Barry's ancestral family. His personal archives of maritime historical data, books, photographs and other artifacts would make a museum curator foam at the mouth. He has been a sounding board, source of data and a kind friend for over twenty years. Barry and his wife, Sylvia, were co-founders of the annual Cape Cod Maritime History Symposium, now in its nineteenth year at the Cape Cod Museum of Natural History. Excuse the colloquial term "bunch," but a bunch of us from Cape Cod had journeyed to Mystic, Connecticut, every year for the annual Mystic Seaport Maritime Symposium. Included in that group was Orleans historian Bill Quinn, Stan and Bonnie Snow of Orleans, Susan Klein of Sandwich, Admont Clark of Dennis and a few others. "Why aren't we doing a similar symposium on Cape Cod?" was the refrain, and so, our very first symposium was in 1997 at Cape Cod Community College. The second year, we began hosting the symposium at the former Sheraton Hotel in Hyannis, where it continued for many years. One symposium year was spent at the Cape Cod Maritime Museum, and since then, at least six years and going, the symposium has been at the Natural History Museum.

Years ago, long before both men died, Admont and Bill had moved on from the symposium, but they kept active writing books and lecturing. Susan Klein, a former director of Sturgis Library, wasn't active in the symposium beyond the first few years. But Bonnie and Stan Snow, along with Barry, have continued their support of and interest in this event that is a key part of Cape Maritime Days held every spring. Through the years, many representatives from various historical societies pitched in and gave great lectures at the symposium, including Eleanor Hammond of the Bourne Historical Society, an expert on the Aptucxet Trading Post. When Dr. John Roche of Harwich was alive, he delivered a few lectures as well; one talk was on the Brooks Academy. So many other historians on Cape Cod have been generous with their time and talent over the years, including David Wright of the Wellfleet Historical Society.

Bonnie Snow is to Orleans what Phyllis Horton is to Dennis. Her knowledge of local history is borne from decades of professional-grade volunteer work in that Lower Cape town. She knows every nuance of yesteryear. She simply knows everything about everything in Orleans.

Many years ago, I met a man named Noel W. Beyle of Eastham. We had never worked together, but we shared an adventure in the offices of the *Yarmouth Register* newspaper. For generations, the *Register* was independently owned, and I used to compose a regular column. When it was bought out, the new corporate owners came in and lined up dozens of boxes containing original copies bound for the incinerator. I was incensed, and so was Noel. I can't remember how we connected, but we met up at the offices to rescue the cartons of original editions for safekeeping. The boxes ended up with Noel, and it's a testament to his character and commitment to history that he cared so much to conserve those first-edition copies.

One of my many regrets is that I didn't get to know Bainbridge Crist better. We had become friends through the Historical Society of Old Yarmouth and had seen each other at events. Crist, Harvard class of '32, was always a dignified presence. He kept his father's ancestral home on Bass River's Pleasant Street, where his daughter, Ann, lives today. Bainbridge passed on many years ago but is a treasured memory among fellow historians.

Lawrence T. Perera, Esq., of Yarmouth Port, a descendant of the Thacher clan that helped found the town of Yarmouth, composed *The Homestead Saga, The Story of a Yarmouth Family and Their Home, 1639–2012*. This book should be required reading for anyone interested in this town's history. And anything that Carlo D'Este composes should be on your reading list, too. Carlo, who lives in Marstons Mills, is one of this country's foremost authorities in military history. He's been a generous mentor to me.

The trajectory of preserving Cape Cod history forever changed when Ben Muse, founder and owner of Parnassus Books in Yarmouth Port, died on July 15, 2012. Ben was in touch with an entire network of people who write about or preserve history. Once he called me to say, "Hey, I've got this book you really need to buy," and sure enough, it was exactly what I needed for research purposes. Ben was intuitive like that. His son, Ben Jr. (who doesn't really go by Jr. but I say so here for distinction purposes), has crafted an ingenious website on Cape Cod history that's available at benmuse.typepad.com. Check it out.

If you've ever gone into Parnassus, you'll know how special this place is. Parnassus is located on Main Street in a nineteenth-century building where used books, as well as new ones, are sold. I'll leave it there because I don't want to sound like a commercial. But I will add that it took a good ten years before Ben allowed me to peek in on the second floor that is closed to the public. It's where all his unsold treasures are: books, manuscripts and other materials. It's breathtaking.

And so this is where I leave you, reader, along my twenty-year journey in Cape Cod history. It's been quite the expedition, with, as the adage says, many miles to go. One last note: if you're ever looking for a worthy cultural cause to which to donate, look no further than the nearest historical society.

Selected Bibliography

In the late nineteenth century, two seminal authors laid the bedrock of historical research on which we heavily rely today, whether new writers, seasoned curators of Cape Cod history or professional or amateur historians.

In 1858, Frederick Freeman published *The History of Cape Cod: The Annals of Barnstable County and of Its Several Towns*. In two volumes, Freeman had captured the larger themes and smaller nuances of English settlement through the late 1800s of what we now know as Cape Cod. Freeman's work was followed in 1890 by Simeon L. Deyo's nearly four-inch-thick *History of Barnstable County, Massachusetts*.

I have relied on these books for the past twenty-five years. These two authors were leaders in compiling formal chronologies of Cape Cod history. If you're new to historical research or want to compile a core library of Cape Cod history books, works by Freeman and Deyo are ones I'd highly recommend as first core purchases. They are printed on acid-free paper with hardcover bindings in Class A archival quality, and the works are meant to last for generations.

For this book, I have relied on over twenty-five years of immersion into local history for many facts and story ideas. Other books and sources, including interviews, whether in person or by telephone and e-mail, were equally helpful.

Some essays were easy to research, like "There's No Place Like Home" or the short theme on trees. Others, not so much. The most challenging was the hidden history of railroads. Because railroad companies merged and changed corporate names over the years, keeping data correctly aligned was arduous. I'm especially grateful to Bill Reidy and Carl Harrison of the Cape Cod Chapter of the National Railway Historical Society for reviewing a final draft of that particular essay.

I've learned my best sources were self-taught historians who have spent a lifetime in devoted and directed research usually revolving around their ancestral families. You'll notice that sources cited include individuals whose depth of knowledge is practically inherent.

What distinguishes historical research from other disciplines, such as hard science, is an expansive bibliography that extends beyond mainstream online databases, books and articles. Human repositories of intelligence are heavy in nuance, perception and interpretation. This type of source complements the local inventory of mainstream knowledge, such as fixed dates of known events. Along the natural course of things, many of these individuals are aging, but these unique sources are recording or writing down what they know. This will certainly help those historians who are coming up through the local ranks. As both a writer and a person, I treasure these contacts, most of whom are in their seventies and eighties. It's critical to remember that most of their grandparents were products of nineteenth-century Cape Cod, so their firsthand view of yesteryear is from eyewitness accounts rather than mere passed-down family lore. Their grandparents' grandparents are the cultural forerunners to Cape Cod of the eighteenth century and even into earlier centuries, so key stories and facts are passed down responsibly as well. Hearing these family tales that descend from generation to generation is to reveal a history that no textbook can hope to capture.

History is subjective, much like love is in the eyes of the beholder. Journalists and historians research and compose subjects that interest us or at least about which we are intensely curious. This is why there's a quirky essay in this book on these botanical sentinels. More than likely you will not find such an essay by another writer who's seeking the hidden history of boats, for instance.

History is dynamic. Past events may remain in a bygone and fixed timeframe. But the way historians process and interpret former eras is in constant motion as new diagnostic technologies come on the market, fresh sources come to light and enlightened perspectives and approaches to study the past evolve, from universities to local historical societies.

I have chosen to pursue those hidden aspects of Cape Cod's much-reviewed history that I felt were most important to a reader, based on my own experience. But another writer who would have composed a similar book in 1975 would most likely choose an entirely different cadre of stories and subjects, as would someone who will write a similar book in, say, 2025.

Newspapers

Barnstable Patriot
Boston Globe
Cape Cod Times
Harwich Independent
Yarmouth Register
Yarmouth Register and Barnstable County Advertiser

Books and Pamphlets

Braginton-Smith, Jack, and Duncan Oliver. *Cape Cod Shore Whaling: America's First Whalemen*. Charleston, SC: The History Press, 2008.

Brooks, Sidney. *Our Village in Three Volumes*. Harwich, MA: Harwich Historical Society, n.d.

Cutler, Carl C. *Important Types of Merchant Sailing Craft*. Mystic, CT: Marine Historical Association, Inc., 1930.

Derick, Burton N., ed. *Dennis Source Records*. Vol. 1, *Church Records*. Dennis, MA, 2004.

Deyo, Simeon. *History of Barnstable County, Massachusetts*. New York: H.W. Blake & Co., 1890.

Dorn, Kay, ed. *Painting a Time: The Diary of Caroline Atherton Dugan*. Brewster, MA: Brewster Ladies' Library, 2014.

Freeman, Frederick. *The History of Cape Cod*. Vol. 1. Boston: Rand and Avery, 1858.

George, Albert Joseph, ed. *The Cap'n's Wife: the Diary of Didama Kelley Doane of West Harwich, Massachusetts*. Syracuse, NY: Syracuse University Press, 1946.

Heath, Dwight B. *Mourt's Relation, A Journal of the Pilgrims at Plymouth*. Bedford, MA: Applewood Books, 1963. First published in 1622.

Hill, Deborah. *Recollections of a Cape Cod Mariner, Elijah Cobb, 1768–1848*. 2nd ed. Brockton, MA: North Road Publishing, 2011.

Holbrook, Charles A., Jr. *History of Old Yarmouth*. Yarmouth Port, MA: Historical Society of Old Yarmouth, 1975.

Keene, Betsey D. *History of Bourne from 1622 to 1937*. Bourne, MA: Bourne Historical Society, Inc. Reprint, 1975.

Mahoney, Haynes R. *Yarmouth's Proud Packets*. West Barnstable, MA: Historical Society of Old Yarmouth, 1986.

Nylander, Jane. *Our Own Snug Fireside, Images of the New England Home, 1760 to 1860*. New Haven, CT: Yale University Press, 1994.

Paine, Josiah. *A History of Harwich, 1620–1800*. N.p.: self-published, 1937.

Perera, Lawrence Thacher. *The Homestead Saga: The Story of a Yarmouth Family and Their Home, 1639–2012*. Yarmouth Port, MA: self-published, 2012.

Rich, Shebnah. *Truro, Cape Cod*. Boston: D. Lothrop and Company, 1883.

Smith, William C. *A History of Chatham, Massachusetts*. Chatham, MA: Chatham Historical Society, Inc., 1971.

Stanger, Margaret A. *That Quail, Robert*. New York: J.B. Lippincott Co., 1966.

Thoreau, Henry David. *Cape Cod*. Boston: Ticknor and Fields, 1865.

Selected Bibliography

Articles and Blogs

Adams, Reverend T.E., Jr. "Mr. Beebe Has Got His Church." *Spritsail* 3, no. 1 (Winter 1989): 2–23.

Craig, Clark. "Cape Cod Gets a War Boom." *Harper's Magazine* (March 1941): 369–74.

Muse, Ben. "Anchor Dragging." March 24, 2010. benmuse.typepad.com/ben_muse.

Historical Societies, Libraries and Universities

Bourne Historical Society
Bridgewater State University
Chatham Historical Library
Falmouth Historical Society
Historical Society of Old Yarmouth
Yarmouth Port Library

Interviews

Carlson, Robert E. Interview with author. E-mail. Cape Cod, MA, February 26, 2015.

Coleman, Nina. Interview with author. E-mail. Cape Cod, MA, January 24, 2015.

Cubellis, Emilio John "E.J.," II. Interview with author. Cape Cod, MA, February 17, 2015.

Cummings, William. Interview with author. E-mail. Cape Cod, MA, February 10, 2015.

Downey, John M. Interview with author. Telephone. Cape Cod, MA, February 26, 2015.

Dunford, Frederick, Jr., PhD. Interview with author. E-mail. Cape Cod, MA, March 5, 2015.

Fone, Heather E. Interview with author. E-mail. Cape Cod, MA, February 24, 2015.

Hill, Deborah. Interview with author. E-mail. Cape Cod, MA, March 3, 2015.

Horton, Phyllis. Interview with author. Telephone. Cape Cod, MA, February 25, 2015.

Kelleher, Thomas. Interview with author. Telephone. Cape Cod, MA, March 4, 2015.

Pokras, Mark, DVM. Interview with author. Cape Cod, MA, March 7, 2015.

Reidy, William. Interview by author. Cape Cod, MA, November 11, 2014.

Ryder, Richard. Interview by author. E-mail. Cape Cod, MA, January 26, 2015.

Shoemaker, Nancy V. Interview by author. E-mail. Cape Cod, MA, February 27, 2015.

Snow, Bonnie. M. Interview by author. Telephone. Cape Cod, MA, March 4, 2015.

Wastrom, Amanda. Interview by author. Personal. Falmouth, MA, February 13, 2015.

Webster, W. Russell. Interview by author. E-mail. Cape Cod, MA, February 26, 2015.

Wright, David. Interview by author. Telephone. Cape Cod, MA, February 24, 2015.

Index

INDEX

About the Author

Theresa Mitchell Barbo writes books in historical nonfiction and frequently lectures before audiences in academic, civic and military circles throughout New England.

She holds BA and MA degrees from the University of Massachusetts–Dartmouth. A native of the Midwest, Theresa resides with her family in Yarmouth Port, a village on the north side of Cape Cod.

Visit her website at theresambarbo.com.